Financing the Capital Requirements of the U.S. Airline Industry in the 1980s

Financing the Capital Requirements of the U.S. Airline Industry in the 1980s

Robert W. Mandell

Lexington Books
D.C. Heath and Company
Lexington, Massachusetts
Toronto

Library of Congress Cataloging in Publication Data

Mandell, Robert W.
  Financing the capital requirements of the U.S. airline industry in the
1980s.

  Bibliography: p.
  Includes index.
  1. Aeronautics, Commercial—United States—Finance. 2. Air
lines—United States—Finance. I. Title.
HE9803.A5M36   387.7'1'0973   79-7747
ISBN 0-669-03215-8

International Standard Book Number: 0-669-03215-8

Library of Congress Catalog Card Number: 79-7747

To William T. Hogan, S.J.
for his guidance and encouragement.

Contents

List of Tables

Introduction

In 1976, a survey was conducted to determine consumer ratings for twenty industries in the United States. Airlines received the highest ranking, while railroads scored the lowest. To the average consumer the two industries appeared to be at the opposite pole of every performance criterion. Airline travel reflected the most dramatic technical accomplishments of twentieth century civilization. Railroads represented obsolescence, financial failure, and physical decay. Comparisons nonetheless were drawn, and the similarities between these two modes of transportation appeared more relevant than the distinctions. They were both in financial trouble.

Traditional lenders are apprehensive about deepening their role in airline financing. A brokerage report published in 1976 bore this ominous title: *Domestic Trunk Airlines: A Shortage Industry In The Making.* The retiring chief executive of Trans World Airlines, a respected business leader, predicted years of shortage, uncertainty, and ultimate bankruptcy for several of the nation's large carriers.[2] A concensus appears to have emerged that the U.S. airline industry will be unable to finance its needs in the coming decade.

The forces giving rise to this concensus came painfully into focus with the difficulties encountered in financing the equipment delivered during the early 1970s. These aircraft, which included the larger and commensurately more expensive B-747's, DC-10's, and L-1011's were acquired only at the expense of intricate financing arrangements that have militated against profitability and, in certain cases, have impaired corporate solvency.

Chapter 2 examines in detail the evolution of the industry's problems as they manifested themselves in the 1970s. The issue giving rise to this study, however, may be stated quite simply. The airline industry's capital requirements are expected to grow as rapidly as those of American industry as a whole. Its capacity to generate an adequate return on that capital, however, is lacking. Internally generated funds are miniscule relative to needs. Depreciation charges based on historical cost bear no similarity to asset replacement cost, since aircraft have risen in price at an annual rate of about 10 percent over the past decade.[3]

In the January 1976 issue of *Forbes*, thirty industries were ranked according to their return on investment. The average for U.S. industry was 8.6 percent. Airlines were last with 3.5 percent. A 1971 article foresaw this dilemma:

> Estimates of requirements for new private capital investment in transportation . . . are all very large in comparison with past experience. . . . [The] earnings records of investor-owned transportation, particularly the railroads and airlines, in terms of return on investment or of stability, compare unfavorably with those of industrial or utility companies.[4]

In 1976 the Air Transport Association (ATA) singled out capital availability as the single largest hurdle to be overcome if the industry is to continue to offer a high level of service: "The greatest obstacle to the future growth and success of the airlines is their unequal stance in the competition for investment funds in a limited capital market."[5]

The airline industry's capital needs will be triple in the 1980s what they were in the 1970s, continuing the logic developed by the Air Transport Association. The same relationship has been estimated for American industry as a whole.[6] The profit margin on sales for the airlines, however, was only about 1.5 percent for the last decade, whereas the rate for manufacturing approximated 5 percent during the same period.[7]

Investment in the 1960s was primarily for the replacement of propeller aircraft. In the 1970s purchases were largely to meet the growth in demand for air travel. In the 1980s aircraft must be acquired for both replacement and growth. Clouding the issue is the fact that between 1976 and the early 1980s there are expected to be abnormally low capacity requirements. This stems from clustered capacity purchases in the past, and excess capacity acquired in the 1971-1975 period, an excess that will have evaporated by 1980 at the very latest.

Why should the economic problems of the industry be a cause for policy concern, and why at this early date? The answers to these questions have several facets.

First, the industry has since its inception been recognized as having many of the characteristics of a public utility. There is a history of public commitment to air transportation as a basic and necessary service. In addition, aircraft manufacturers typically require at least two years for aircraft delivery, and perhaps as long as five years for aircraft development (such as the forthcoming Boeing 7X7). Boeing will only accept orders from financially sound airlines, and only three of the nation's five largest carriers are deemed to be within this favored catetory.[8] Failure to place orders on a timely basis will imply (1) shortages for the traveler; and (2) failure to embody new technologies in the radically altered aircraft designs geared to foster operating economies.

The timing of capacity requirements is of particular importance with respect to the related question of whether or not the next generation of aircraft will ever be built. If they are, will their development come soon enough to fill the gaps in tomorrow's fleet before these gaps are filled with planes embodying older technologies? This point is particularly crucial, because if the industry waits until a shortage is in progress, it will opt for aircraft that are available in the shortest possible time. The danger arises that the industry will be locked into a significant amount of relatively obsolete and inefficient equipment for an extended period, during which operating economies will become ever more crucial.

The aircraft manufacturers—like the institutional investors—have grown cautious because of the uncertainties currently surrounding the airline industry. While the railroad industry encountered its difficulties over a period of secular stagnation in the demand for rail service, the airline industry has developed its problems in a climate of continued growth and expansion. While the reasons are many and complex, a significant factor has been that aircraft tend to be ordered in relatively large groups, are delivered together over a relatively short span of time, and tend to create overcapacity until growth can absorb them.

Purchases are clustered because of the development of new aircraft at a given point in time. The large-scale delivery of the jumbo jets in the early 1970s, for example, will lead to large-scale replacement needs in the late 1980s. Furthermore, airlines place orders for aircraft in years when financial performance is relatively strong. These are years of optimism when corporate liquidity favors such commitments and aircraft manufacturers have confidence in the airlines' ability to pay upon delivery.

The purpose of this study is to determine whether or not the eleven largest U.S. airlines (the domestic trunk carriers and Pan American) can finance their capital needs in the 1980s.[9] The specific objectives will be as follows:

1. To determine by year and company capital requirements for expansion and aircraft replacement under alternative assumptions. While emphasis will be placed on the period ending in 1989, the study will estimate capital needs through the entire fleet replacement cycle ending in 1994.
2. To estimate the funds available, internally and through external financing, for investment in new aircraft.
3. To propose policy measures based on these findings.

The task is facilitated by the fact that the industry is a regulated one. Every vital statistic of the subject companies is open to public scrutiny on the Form 41's of the respective carriers, a comprehensive document filed periodically with the Civil Aeronautics Board (CAB).

The issues to be confronted are so large that a step back in time will lend a useful perspective to the questions at hand. The first chapter takes this brief journey through the history of the industry, stopping analytically at those points that bear greatest significance to the present status of the industry.

Notes

1. Donaldson, Lufkin, and Jenrette, *Domestic Trunk Airlines: A Shortage Industry in The Making* (New York: Donaldson, Lufkin, and Jenrette, 1976).
2. Charles Tillinghast, *Aviation Daily*, December 9, 1976.
3. See table 3-26.
4. John L. Weller, "Access to Capital Markets," for the American Assembly

in *The Future of American Transportation*, E.W. Williams, ed. (New Jersey: Prentice-Hall, Inc., 1971). Reprinted with permission.

5. Air Transport Association, *The Sixty Billion Dollar Question*, (ATA Press, 1976), p. 6. Reprinted with permission.

6. Ibid., p. 6.

7. Ibid., p. 6.

8. James Woolsey and James Baumgarner, "Airplane Builders Prepare Assault on Economic Barrier," in *Air Transport World*, February 1978.

9. These include American, Braniff, Continental, Delta, Eastern, National, Northwest, Pan American, Trans World, United, and Western.

1

Highlights of the Industry's Development (1914-1970)

Efficient transportation is vital to the functioning of a specialized, industrial society. In nineteenth century America, railroads served to channel the pulse of an expanding nation. In the twentieth century, this role has devolved to the nation's highways and to its airlines. The following is a synopsis of the latter; its evolution and its achievements; its status and its difficulties.

The first scheduled air service in the United States was the St. Petersburg-Tampa Airboat Line, which began and ended service on January 1 and March 1 of 1914. In spite of its brief existence, its record amazed many of those who were skeptical about the commercial merits of the airplane.[1] Some 1,274 passengers traveled the twenty-one miles across Tampa Bay and back for the ten dollars without injury or loss of life.

In 1916 the United States government became formally involved in the fledgling industry for the first time. The Post Office Department signed a contract with various private operators for the delivery of mail, and in 1918 airmail delivery came directly under the control of that agency.[2]

Between June and December of 1927, the postal department released control of its forty-three pilots, its planes, and six-hundred ground employees to serve in the newly formed airlines. Twelve million aircraft miles had been flown between 1918 and 1927 at a cost of $17.5 million. This was partially offset by $5 million postage paid. The $12.5 million apparent deficit was a small price to pay for establishing commercial aviation.[3]

In 1926 the Kelly Act became law, whereby government committed itself to the development of air transportation. Probably the most important feature of the 1926 law was that it "charged the federal government with the operation and maintenance of the airway system, as well as all aids to navigation, and to provide safety in air commerce generally through a system of regulation."[4]

One of the industry's leading historians goes a step further, indicating that "the modern airline system can be dated from the Kelly Act, because the carriers awarded those initial four year contracts eventually became part of United, American, and Trans World, the largest of the permanent domestic companies."[5] The climactic steps leading to the present system, however, were embodied in the Airmail Act of 1930, and ultimately in the Civil Aeronautics Act of 1938.

The time is now April 29, 1930, the day on which the Airmail Act of that year—the so-called McNary Watres Act—was passed by Congress. Supported by the Hoover administration, the act is generally pointed to as ushering in the second phase in the chronicle of U.S. commercial aviation. The 1930 act was

1

largely the work of one very powerful and controversial cabinet officer in the Hoover administration: Postmaster General Walter Brown.[6]

To this day, Brown is alternatively praised and vilified. He wanted a system of three large self-supporting transcontinental airlines, whose main business was to be passenger carriage and not mail conveyance. According to some authors, "in a meeting with airline leaders, Brown encouraged them to develop a profitable passenger business, and in this manner become independent of the subsidy of mail contracts."[7] The 1930 act gave Brown "dictatorial powers over the airline industry; therefore commercial aviation took on the characteristics of a federally regulated industry."[8] To foster the development and acquisition of passenger aircraft, Brown developed a new basis for airmail payments to the carriers, "a charter system; the government paid for the entire airplane, not just for the mail being airlifted."[9] This obviously encouraged the purchase of large passenger aircraft.

Brown forced the airlines to use cabin attendants for passengers, extended or consolidated routes at will, and told the many small airlines that contracts would go only to a few large carriers. A rush to merge occurred, and three large entities emerged: United, American, and Trans World Airlines. The remaining smaller companies were left out. "To them it meant no mail contract and no contract meant going out of business. Brown therefore got the large transcontinental airline companies that he wanted."[10] One injured party took his case to prominent democrats who were likely to be influential if the Hoover administration failed to return to office in 1932. His name was Tom Braniff.

When Brown left office, thirty-four airmail routes were in existence, costing the government 54 cents per mile, down from $1.10 per mile when Brown took office. In summary, "the results were good if no attention was paid to those who had been trampled upon."[11]

But attention was paid to Brown's questionable ethics, and pressure to redress grievances became intense on the incoming Roosevelt administration. Postmaster General Farley accused the air carriers of collusion with Brown, cancelled the contracts, and ordered the ill-equipped air corps to take over delivery of the mail on February 19, 1934. The results were nothing short of disastrous.

The per mile cost increased from 54 cents to $2.21.[12] In other terms, the record was even worse: "Finally after 66 crashes, 12 deaths, and a cost to the government of nearly four million dollars, President Roosevelt ordered the army to cease flying the airmail on June 1, 1934, after nearly six months' operation."[13] The Supreme Court later awarded $2.5 million to the airlines for Farley's breach of contract.[14]

A postscript to this incident was the Airmail Act of 1934. It attempted to restore the competitive bidding process usurped by Brown. Farley swore that no contract would be awarded to companies he accused of conspiring with Brown. The result bordered on the absurd. The same companies obtained the contracts, but altered their names: "The three airlines had disguised themselves by changing their names slightly; American Airways became American Airlines, Eastern Air Transport became Eastern Airlines, and Transcontinental and Western Air just added the suffic 'Inc.' "[15]

The 1934 act gave three agencies regulatory control. The Interstate Commerce Commission fixed rates; the Post Office was to see only to the requirements of the mails; and the Department of Commerce would set and enforce safety standards through its Bureau of Air Commerce (later to become the Federal Aviation Administration).

The regulatory lines of demarcation were not clearly drawn, however, and confusion soon arose. Mail rates were controlled, but passenger rates were not. The 1934 act indicated that subsequent to 1938, government payments to the airlines could not exceed postage revenues. The development of new aircraft promised significant technological advances to the traveling public. But with price cutting among the airlines to attract passengers, and mail payments limited to postage revenues, "the airlines could not have afforded the newer and larger airplanes within such limitations."[16]

The Civil Aeronautics Act of 1938 defined the domestic airline industry and the firms that comprise it. A "certificate of convenience and necessity" was to be required for operating an airline. According to Section 401(e) of that act, carriers who had provided adequate and continuous airmail service from May 14 to August 22, 1938 would receive a permanent certificate of convenience and necessity, revocable only for violation of other provisions of the law.[17] Airlines so designated were the following:

American Airlines

Braniff Airways

Chicago and Southern Airlines

Continental Airlines

Delta Air Corporation

Northwest Airlines

Pennsylvania Central Airlines

Transcontinental & Western Air

Inland Airlines

Mid-Continent Airlines

National Airlines

Northeast Airlines

United Air Lines

Western Air Express

Wilmington-Catalina Airlines

Of these fifteen carriers, six have vanished through mergers and reorganizations. Chicago and Southern and Northeast Airlines merged with Delta, Inland with Western, and Mid-Continent with Braniff. Pennsylvania was renamed Capital and subsequently merged with United. Transcontinental and Western became Trans World Airlines.[18]

Conspicuously absent from the discussion thus far has been the only international carrier prior to World War II, Pan American Airways. Prior to the advent of the CAB, a working relationship existed between the government, particularly the military, and the U.S. flag carrier. In the mid 1920s, a German-controlled Colombian airline bid to carry mail between the United States and Latin America. Major Henry Arnold, later to be chief of the Army Air Force, drew up a prospectus for a company to be called Pan American. Juan Trippe—founder of the company—secured exclusive landing rights in Cuba and certain other Latin American destinations. Often assisted by the Department of State, Trippe systematically expanded his operation: "By first securing landing rights from the governments involved, Trippe made certain that none of his potential competitors could provide airmail service. He could then submit airmail bids at the highest allowable rate . . . "[19]

Postmaster Brown settled on Pan American as the one large international carrier he had envisioned. The present structure of Pan American is traceable, as are so many aspects of the industry's structure, to Brown's wishes: "He thus warned [Pan American Airways] and domestic companies to stay out of each other's markets."[20] The Roosevelt administration denied any partnership with Pan American, although large sums were given to the company in the 1939-1941 period to compete against Italian and German operations in Latin America. Pan American drove a German-controlled Colombian airline into bankruptcy, and bought it at auction with funds obtained from a subsidiary of the Reconstruction Finance Coropration.[21]

In World War II, the domestic airlines, including Pan American, were fully mobilized in the war effort. The success of this effort has led many today to advocate airline financing through an industry-military partnership. With this approach, the government would assist individual companies in obtaining their needed capital, and the companies would come under military jurisdiction in times of national emergency. Proponents of this approach have not put forth a specific plan, and the merits of such an approach are far from clear.

Before 1946 airports were financed by local governments. As aviation needs became more sophisticated, the majority of communities were priced out of the market for new airport construction. In response to this, the government enacted the Federal Airport Act of 1946. Under its terms, localities could obtain 50 to 100 percent of needed construction funds from the federal government.

The Airport and Airways Development Act of 1970 had a similar goal, this time financing its aims through (1) a percentage tax on domestic airline travel; (2) a flat charge on international flights originating in the United States; and (3) an annual aircraft registration tax.

The Federal Aviation Act of 1958 made few changes in the economic regulation of the industry. It was passed in response to three mid-air collisions, and aimed to replace the highly constrained Civil Aeronautics Administration with an unhampered and more powerful body, the Federal Aviation Agency. In 1966 all airline regulatory bodies came under the purview of the newly created Department of Transportation.

For the international carrier, the period following World War II was a different one in many ways. The so-called "fifth freedom" was the pivotal topic of negotiations among Western nations after the war. The first freedom is the right to overfly another country's airspace without landing. The second is to land only for fuel and repairs, without offering passenger or cargo service. The third freedom is the right to carry traffic from the country of the airline's nationality to the foreign nation, and the fourth freedom is the right to convey passengers from the foreign country to the airline's home country. The fifth freedom is "the right to carry traffic which neither originated in, nor is destined for, the home country of the airline."[22]

The Bermuda Agreement was a sweeping departure from previous ones in that it granted unlimited fifth freedom rights to all carriers:

> It substitutes a sweeping right of each airline to institute capacity in its own discretion and to carry fifth freedom traffic in its own discretion . . . subject only to *ex post facto* action if a government complains that the capacity violates certain general principles . . .[23]

Other nations subsidize their international flag carriers for a myriad of economic and political reasons. Many European nations do so to foster tourism and to prevent the foreign exchange drain which would result if their citizens were to fly on the airlines of other nations. Underdeveloped nations may wish to capitalize on what Raul Prebisch refers to as technological density—the high technology skills which accompany the development of a sophisticated industry.

Whatever the reason, the American flag carrier is at a disadvantage vis-à-vis its foreign competition. One critic of this imbalance indicates that, "The illogical outcome of all this is that the government holds that it cannot help U.S. airlines because they are private enterprises but it must hurt them in the national interest."[24]

Typical of this issue was the threat made by the Dutch to cease contributing to the North Atlantic Treaty Organization (NATO) until major concessions were granted to KLM, the Dutch national airline. An estimate appearing in the *New York Times* on April 1, 1957 held that the Dutch could earn fifteen dollars within the United States for every dollar American carriers could earn in Holland. The Congress and Senate pointed out that the U.S. international carriers were never consulted before the United States government offered concessions to foreign air carriers.

In 1961 President John F. Kennedy appointed a "generally nonpartisan" group, the Project Horizon Task Force, to study past American policy in granting such concessions. The task force concluded that: "the U.S. should be more cautious in the future, especially where the richest markets are at stake."[25]

Pan American tried repeatedly to have itself established as the uncontested U.S. flag carrier. In 1944 the McCarran Bill sought to establish the All American Flag Line, Inc. Alarmed at this prospect, the domestic airlines bitterly opposed the bill. The administration did also, and achieved a Congressional stalemate. During this deadlock, the executive branch made several moves to thwart Pan American's vision. Trans World Airlines (TWA) was named to fly certain Atlantic routes. American Airlines was given several overseas routes, and was renamed American Overseas Airlines. In 1950 American petitioned President Truman to sell these routes to Pan American. The president agreed, but awarded several additional routes to TWA so that competition would not suffer.[26]

In 1962, Pan American and TWA requested permission to form one overseas company, with Pan American as the basic surviving entity. TWA was in serious financial trouble, but many remained skeptical: "Some observers interpreted the move only as the latest attempt by [Pan American] to make itself the U.S. chosen instrument in world aviation"[27] TWA's financial condition improved, and the request was dropped.

Indeed, the fortunes of most carriers looked promising in the first half of the 1960s. The introduction of jet aircraft reduced cost, enhanced safety, and promoted business and pleasure travel. Fuel costs were stable, wage increases were manageable, consumer demand strong, and financial performance apparently adequate. This climate showed no clear signs of imminent danger, and no danger was perceived. Projections of industry growth became increasingly optimistic. When Boeing, Douglas, and Lockheed announced plans to develop their respective jumbo jets, the individual airlines feared only that their competitors would acquire the new aircraft before themselves. Projections of future travel demand became more and more optimistic, and aircraft orders were placed accordingly. With expectations for a boundless future, leverage was seen as an appropriate technique for maximizing stockholders' profits.

But before the first 747's rolled off the assembly line a recession was in progress, and a financial debacle became inevitable.

Notes

1. Robert M. Kane and Allan D. Vose, *Air Transportation* (Dubuque: Kendall/Hunt Publishing Co., 1974), p. 121.

2. Frederick C. Thayer, *Air Transport Policy and National Security: A Political, Economic, and Military Analysis* © 1965 The University of North Carolina Press, p. 3.

3. Kane and Vose, *Air Transportation*, p. 26.

4. Ibid., p. 28.

5. Thayer, *Air Transport Policy*, p. 7. Reprinted with permission.

6. Kane and Vose, *Air Transportation*, p. 30.

7. Ibid., p. 30.

8. Ibid., p. 30.

9. Thayer, *Air Transport Policy*, p. 10. Reprinted with permission.

10. Kane and Vose, *Air Transportation*, p. 31.

11. Ibid., p. 31.

12. Ibid.

13. Ibid.

14. Kane and Vose, *Air Transportation*, p. 33.

15. Ibid., p. 33.

16. Thayer, *Air Transport Policy*, p. 17. Reprinted with permission.

17. Kane and Vose, *Air Transportation*, p. 35.

18. Kane and Vose, *Air Transportation*, p. 36.

19. Thayer, *Air Transport Policy*, p. 34. Reprinted with permission.

20. Henry Ladd Smith, *Airways Abroad* (Madison: University of Wisconsin Press, 1950), p. 59.

21. Thayer, *Air Transport Policy*, p. 34.

22. William E. O'Connor, *Economic Regulation of the World's Airlines*, p. 14. © 1971 by William E. O'Connor. Reprinted with permission of Holt, Rinehart and Winston.

23. O'Connor, *Economic Regulation of the World's Airlines*, p. 14. Reprinted with permission.

24. Kane and Vose, *Air Transportation*, p. 79. Reprinted with permission.

25. U.S. Federal Aviation Agency, *Report of the Task Force on Aviation Goals* (Washington: Government Pub. Office, 1961), p. 116.

26. Thayer, *Air Transport Policy*, p. 276.

27. Thayer, *Air Transport Policy*, p. 276.

2 Crisis in the 1970s: A Financial Overview

In the years following the Aviation Act of 1938, the industry grew rapidly. Passengers enplaned on U.S. carriers climbed at a compound rate of growth of over 15 percent per year between 1938 and 1972.[1] Revenue passenger miles climbed at a compound rate of over 17 percent during these years.[2] Yet by the end of this period there prevailed a general sentiment that something major was going wrong.

It is a commonplace of economic theory that, over the long run, a certain minimal return on investment is required to secure capital for any given employment. Marginal differentials in the rate of return restore equilibrium between the marginal productivities of capital in its many applications.

In addition to such marginal adjustments, however, the long-run failure of an industry or firm to generate a sufficient return on capital leads to quantum changes in its ability to survive. This is reallocation in the sense of creative destruction—the cataclysmic process of corporate struggle portrayed by Schumpeter, not the infinitely divisible steps toward general equilibrium envisioned by Ricardo and Marshall.

While difficulties in an industry may appear to be precipitated by a sudden, immediate crisis, paroxysm is generally preceded by a period of chronic—though perhaps subtle—malaise. The Penn Central bankruptcy typifies this process. Though failure took the financial community and the investing public largely by surprise, the underlying factors were chronic for many years.

When the Air Transport Association drew a systematic comparison between the airlines and the railroads in 1975, the conclusion was shocking: the railroads, on the whole, were doing better financially. In 1972, however, the trend of analysis was more introspective, as seen in this statement made by the ATA:

> The airlines are in trouble. In 1970, despite stern cost-cutting, they lost about $100 million. While 1970 was a recession year when practically all industries did poorly, airlines fared relatively worse than most. The following year, the industry barely broke even.[3]

The ATA further pointed out that the weakness in the industry had prevailed for many years prior to surfacing dramatically in 1970. In the 1960s two factors helped to obscure the industry's underlying problems. The first was growth. Not only did intercity public travel increase, but so did the domestic airlines' share of it—from about 48 percent in 1962 to over 75 percent in 1971. The second element was the single greatest large-scale innovation in the history of commercial aviation: the introduction of jet-powered aircraft. This unquestionably was "a major technological innovation whose efficiencies produced enormous cost benefits for the industry."[4]

By 1970, however, rising costs stemming from the general inflation "overtook and passed benefits gained by converting from propeller to jet fleets."[5] On the revenue side, the recession reduced 1970 passenger traffic by 1 percent from 1969, after growing by 10 percent and 15 percent in 1968 and 1969, respectively. The 1971 traffic increased by only 1.9 percent over that in 1970.[6]

Every category of costs appeared to be out of control. Even landing fees climbed by 105 percent between 1965 and 1969 for identical aircraft. Many communities began to view these fees as a costless way to raise revenue: "In effect, airlines are at the mercy of monopoly landlords and are unable to bargain effectively to protect themselves and the public."[7]

Between 1962 and 1970 the industry almost held its own. Operating revenues grew an impressive 278.8 percent. Operating expenses, however, climbed 287.6 percent. By 1970 the plight of the domestic trunk carriers became obvious. Their combined 1970 operating loss was $100 million. Revenue passenger miles decreased 1 percent from 1969, while operating expenses climbed by 10.8 percent. The 52 percent load factor was the lowest in recent history. This declined even further to 50.2 percent in 1971.[8]

The rate of return approached zero. Commitments previously made for the purchase of aircraft were about to come due. The 747's and DC-10's were beginning to enter the marketplace, providing exactly what was not needed—new capacity on an unprecedented scale. The fear of years before that the airline industry could not go it alone was echoed once more. Dark references were made comparing the problems of the airline industry to the plight of the railroads.

While revenue passenger miles increased about three and one-half times between 1960 and 1970, interest charges went up nearly five times, and interest on long-term debt was over 44 percent higher in 1971 than 1968. Three factors combined to make this category of expense rise so dramatically. First, interest rates were rising generally. Second, and more important, reequipment became necessary, and years of inadequate earnings forced the airlines to "rely to an abnormal degree on borrowing."[9] The third factor was a growing awareness on the part of the financial community that airlines posed a distinct credit risk, and their consequent insistence on a risk premium to compensate for it.

Another obstacle confronting the industry is a price setting mechanism that moves with all the ponderous complication that bureaucracy can contrive. The CAB has developed a highly involved formula for computing the allowed rate of return. Many adjustments are made to actual costs and investments incurred by the companies to disallow items not deemed to be in keeping with regulatory policy.

One of these adjustments relates to aircraft seating configuration. The CAB wants more seats than the airlines as a group have on any type aircraft. A percentage of airline costs and investments are therefore disallowed for rate making. Another adjustment relates to passengers. The CAB holds that at least 55 percent of an aircraft's seats should be occupied by full-fare passengers. This has often proved to be an elusive goal; hence further expense and investment base disallowances. The CAB encourages discount fares, but then disallows an additional portion of investment and operating expenses, "thus resulting in both lower basic fares and lower discount fares than would otherwise be the case."[10]

If airlines attempt to increase load factors by restricting flights at off-peak demand times, another pitfall awaits: the test of aircraft utilization. The airlines have been unable to fly their aircraft as many hours per day as the CAB believes optimal. The result is that "still more investment and operating expenses are disallowed for rate making purposes on the grounds that the airlines purchased too much equipment."[11] The "fair" annual return on investment was set at 10.5 percent from 1961 to 1971, and 12 percent thereafter. From 1961 to 1970 the domestic trunk carriers earned the 10.5 percent only once.[12]

Until recent years the airlines were unwilling to experiment with fare reductions. The CAB has always contended that the price elasticity of demand for air travel is high. The airlines have traditionally held the reverse. Actually, the answer depends on the route in question, the composition of the market (business versus pleasure), the season, and the total price of vacations in alternative tourist markets. While large price reductions may well increase traffic significantly, it has often been demonstrated that small changes in fares have no perceptible impact on the level of traffic.[13]

Conversely, "the elasticity of demand in the tourist market when a substantial fare reduction is offered, is also demonstrated by the history of charter flights, particularly across the Atlantic Ocean."[14] A study by the Port of New York Authority concluded that international business travel increased significantly with reduced travel time, as jet aircraft replaced propeller planes. Apparently, "in 1956, 2,500 business trips were made to Europe by American residents for every billion dollars worth of direct foreign investment. By 1963, the number had increased to 3,700."[15] In domestic markets, the elasticity of demand for business travel tends to be very low, while pleasure traffic is generally price elastic. The extent of this elasticity is not at all clear, however, since "for most travelers the air fare is only a small part of the overall trip expense."[16] In 1970, for the average two week trip to a resort hotel, only 20 percent of the total cost was for air fare.

While there is some ambiguity surrounding price elasticity of demand for air travel in many markets, there is general agreement that the demand for air travel is highly income elastic for all components of the market. A Brookings Institution study indicates that "air travel demand appears highly income elastic, that is it responds disproportionately to given changes in income level."[17] The ATA elaborates on the reasons for this:

> In a recession . . . people tend to postpone pleasure travel. Companies
> tend to cut back on business trips or on the number of people sent on a
> given trip. Fewer people travel first class . . . so that the dollar yields
> realized by airlines is reduced.[18]

Bringing these analytical threads together, one can see a convergence of
problems in the 1970-1971 period. Costs were rising sharply. Fare increases were
not granted. Between 1961 and 1971, the consumer price index had climbed
over 30 percent, but air fares remained unchanged. Uncertain economic
conditions were causing individuals and businesses to retrench. And all this was
happening when airlines were obtaining massive additions to capacity from the
delivery of new aircraft ordered in the late 1960s.

Theoretically, the supply of airline service should be elastic, since a flight
may be cancelled or service reduced to a given destination. In reality, however,
this is far from the case: "as a practical matter an airline finds it a competitive
necessity to maintain its announced schedules and maintain frequent depar-
tures."[19]

Other factors cooperate to make the supply of air service rigid in the short
run. Pilots and crews are paid an annual wage. Aircraft continue to depreciate.
Aircraft must be ordered years in advance of anticipated need. "Furthermore,
the acquisition of new aircraft requires decisions to be made years in advance of
the delivery of the equipment."[20]

Airlines must forecast future demand and hope that when aircraft are
delivered they will be able to fill an adequate number of seats. "When aircraft
are delivered, supply jumps by sudden increments"[21] and there may well be a
period during which load factors are reduced until demand rises and absorbs the
increased supply. Since fixed costs and semi-fixed costs are so high, little can be
saved by reducing the scale of operations in the short run.

Combining the uncertainties in capacity estimation with the rate-making
policies described previously, one is able to discern the basis for the 1970-1971
difficulties and to identify possible links between regulatory policy and possible
equipment shortages in the industry.

If the airlines are on the margin of maintaining load factors required by the
CAB's formula, they will hesitate to order new aircraft if there will be any
period during which the service lives of new and old aircraft overlap. Another
issue concerns the nature of the demand for air travel. It is typically not a
smooth demand, but rather one characterized by sharp seasonal peaks and
valleys. Eastern Airlines, a north-south carrier, does its largest share of business
in the winter. American typically earns one and one-half times the revenue in
August that it does in February. Still another large carrier on a Sunday in June
"flies twice the passenger volume that it does on a February Tuesday."[22]

Airlines must be equipped to handle these peaks, or else disappoint and
inconvenience a significant number of people. There is a very real possibility that

the inability of the scheduled airlines to cope with peak period demand would mean a no-growth situation for the industry. Aging equipment, congested airports, and consumer uncertainty might discourage travel or shift demand to other modes of transportation and, ultimately, further deterioration could result.

The ATA was preoccupied with the peak demand issue in 1971. As new capacity suppressed load factors, the CAB denied rate increases at a time when they were badly needed to offset soaring operating costs. The association indicated that "the peaking problem translates into heavy costs for the industry. To accommodate peak demands, airlines must have the planes, personnel, and ground facilities adequate to the need."[23]

The 1960-1970 period saw pleasure travel expand from about 15 percent to almost half the domestic travel market. It appears, therefore, that the CAB is failing to acknowledge the legitimate right of people to travel when they wish to.

The problems the domestic trunk carriers encountered during the 1970 economic slack were exacerbated by the rapid growth in prior periods. "When growth stops during a recession, an industry which normally has a 15% growth rate is more severely affected than one accustomed to a growth rate of five or six percent."[24]

What the ATA might also have pointed out is that retrenchment is easier for an industry that does not require such large proportions of fixed capital assets and specialized labor to deliver its service.

The period 1970-1971 brought the long-run problems of the industry into focus. Years of inadequate earnings forced the airlines to borrow to the limit to finance the acquisition of new equipment ordered in the late 1960s. As the 727-200's, 747's, and finally DC-10's and L-1011's rolled off the production lines, an additional source of funds became necessary. The airlines found it in leasing.

While the practice of leasing aircraft and related equipment had occurred prior to this time, it was during 1968-1975 that this financing vehicle prospered. In 1970 aircraft rentals for the domestic trunk airlines and Pan American stood at $176.1 million, up an incredible 51.6 percent from $116.1 million just one year earlier.[25]

One reason for the popularity of leasing stems from the investment tax credit. A chronically unprofitable airline could not use the offset to federal income taxes available from capital expenditures that qualified under this provision of the tax law. But a profitable leasing company (with a positive tax liability) could, and would either pass on a portion to the airline lessee in the form of a lower implicit interest charge, or would agree to finance a proposal otherwise denied.

Another and crucially important issue surrounds the legal capacity of a corporation to raise capital. As indicated, many of the airlines had borrowed to the limit. The practical point of reference for this boundary is often dictated by restrictive indentures in covenants with bondholders. These agreements typically set maximum limits to total indebtedness, debt/equity ratios, and encumbrances. While today such leases must be capitalized according to strict specifications laid down by the Financial Accounting Standards Board (see appendix B on leasing), in 1970 such agreements were consigned to financial limbo. Leasing enabled companies who were at the ceiling of permitted borrowings to borrow more.

The airlines survived the 1970-1971 onslaught, but at a high price. Long-term commitments—typically fifteen to eighteen years with implicit interest rates as high as 12 percent—were necessary to survive the early 1970s financing crunch.

The next several years confirmed many of the forebodings of 1970-1971. Many basic expenses began to appear uncontrollable. In 1975, the U.S. domestic trunk airlines flew approximately 25 percent more revenue passenger miles than in 1969, but fuel expense climbed 252.3 percent despite fewer gallons consumed per revenue ton mile.[26] In 1976 the ATA singled out fuel prices as the greatest threat to airline viability. The association indicated that "the average price of jet fuel has increased more than 160 percent, from 12¢ per gallon to the current 32¢ per gallon since mid-1973"[27]

For the domestic trunk and regional airlines, fuel price increases added $1.9 billion to operating expenses between April 1, 1973 and December 31, 1975. Fare increases were, the industry contends, smaller than required, generating only $1.2 billion in offsetting revenues. The resulting shortfall of $700 million served only to deteriorate the already difficult financial picture for the industry. Using the CAB standard for a reasonable rate of return, the 1966-1976 profit shortfall for the domestic trunk carriers was $3.6 billion.[28] Since 1968 the railroads, a perennial reminder of a system gone hopelessly amuck, had actually been enjoying a higher profit margin on sales than the domestic trunk carriers.[29]

Of all regulated industries, airlines are among the riskiest from the investor's point of view, and consequently require a higher rate of return. In fact, however, they earn the lowest. For the years 1962-1975,

> ... the airline industry's return on net assets was about one-half that experienced by investor-owned electric utilities. The financially troubled Class I railroad industry achieved a greater return over this period than did the airlines.[30]

Between 1962 and 1975, the return on net assets for electric utilities averaged 4.1 percent; for Class I railroads 2.6 percent; for airlines 2.4 percent.[31] In January 1976, *Forbes* published an analysis of returns on investment in major U.S. industries for the period 1971-1975. The study revealed that airlines have the lowest rate of return for any major industry.

Traditionally, airlines have raised a significant percentage of their total capitalization through the issuance of common stock. The market price of the domestic trunk airlines' common stock taken as a whole is less than book value, effectively barring new stock offerings. On December 31, 1966 the equity securities of the trunk carriers had a market value of $6.7 billion and a book value of $2.4 billion. Ten years later, the chronically lackluster performance of the industry had taken its toll. "By the third quarter of 1975, the market value had fallen to $2.5 billion and the book value had risen to $4.1 billion."[32]

In 1966 the current portion of long-term debt for the trunk carriers was $42,479,000, approximately 9.4 percent of operating earnings. By 1975 the figure had grown 624 percent and absorbed 20.7 percent of operating earnings. Interest on long-term debt over this ten-year period rose more than 316 percent. Added to this in 1975 was the burden of financing leases, as discussed previously.[33]

Drawing together the many elements touched on defines the central problem confronting the industry, its regulators, and the traveling public. Vast sums will be required over the course of the decade ahead to (1) replace aging aircraft; (2) exploit the operating economies offered by new technology embodied in new capital equipment; and (3) meet the growth anticipated in the demand for air travel.

Militating against this possibility is a chronic lack of profitability, which has closed the door to equity financing; driven indebtedness to the practical limit, both in the form of long-term debt and capital leases; and caused traditional lenders to avoid making commitments to the airline industry. Furthermore, regulatory uncertainty has made lenders fearful that deregulation might cause even thinner profits or even bankruptcy for certain carriers. Many potential lenders are indicating an unwillingness to commit funds until the long-run objectives and scope of regulation are spelled out with complete certainty.

If new aircraft are not acquired by 1984, the 1976 fleet would furnish only half of the demand projected for that date, even at load factors of 60 percent. The development of the next generation of aircraft is only now appearing somewhat certain. It is important that momentum be maintained to have the new aircraft available by 1983-1985 when major purchases will begin to take place. Of the five largest carriers, only Delta, American, and United have the financial credibility to spur the development of new aircraft by placing large orders for a proposed design. The needs of these three carriers, however, are far from identical. American wants the new aircraft to be transcontinental, whereas United's maximum range requirement is to service its Denver-East Coast and Cleveland-West Coast routes. American wants its plane to seat at least 190 and to have three engines for added safety on its over-water routes where the nearest airport may be hours away. United originally wanted the new plane to have 175 seats and to utilize only two engines. The company has since agreed on a larger size aircraft, as discussed in chapter 4. Delta is quite satisfied with the status quo:

In the past four years it has spent a billion dollars building its fleet around the 727-200 and the L-1011. The average age of its airplanes is just five years. . . . Delta has good reason to be impressed with the 727-200. The airplane has been used essentially to replace Convair 880's and non-fan DC-8's and has provided the airline with a 26% improvement in seat miles per gallon of fuel over those airplanes. Delta burned less fuel in 1976 than in 1972 while carrying 38% more passengers.[34]

Boeing is the "only U.S. aircraft manufacturer proposing a new airplane."[35] Lockheed and McDonnell-Douglas have decided instead to offer derivatives of the L-1011 and DC-10. The cost justification for this lies in the massive expenditures required to develop a new aircraft. The B-767 may cost $1.5 billion or more to develop. Lockheed has indicated that the L-1011 will cost only $60 million.[36]

It appears that demand is going to be adequate to spur the development of Boeing's new aircraft. Several years of reasonably promising financial performance will be required, however, for a broad spectrum of the airlines to commit themselves to these new aircraft on a major scale. There is still one factor, however, which is far from clear: the cost feasibility of the new aircraft.

Boeing first estimated that the new aircraft would cost "about $25 million per copy."[37] United's purchase price for the new aircraft was $40 million a piece.[38] As indicated, the cost of developing the 7X7 will be massive. "The 7X7 is the biggest undertaking, requiring about $1.5 billion in development costs and about four years (some have estimated five) from program go-ahead to delivery."[39]

What will the $1.5 billion translate into on a per aircraft basis? Table 2-1

Table 2-1
Potential Demand for The 7X7

	Maximum 7X7 Aircraft Per Year				
Airline	1984	1985	1986	1987	Total
American	25	38	44	40	147
Braniff	7	16	5	8	36
Continental	4	4	12	6	26
Delta	13	13	14	15	55
National	6	6	19	5	36
Eastern	21	26	42	26	115
Northwest	14	12	23	20	69
Pan Am	20	31	24	27	102
TWA	32	30	32	34	128
United	43	48	75	80	246
Western	7	7	15	13	42
Total	192	231	305	274	1,002

uses the forecast of capital requirements developed in chapter 3, and assumes that all capacity purchased in the 1983-1987 period is filled with a 200-seat model of the 757 or 767 aircraft. As the table indicates, the total number of such aircraft that could be absorbed would be 1,002. This assumption is most unrealistic, since 727's, DC-10's, 747's, L-1011's and even European Airbuses will fill many of the requirements during this period. If the $1.5 billion in development costs were spread over all the 1,002 aircraft, the cost of development would be $14.97 million each. If, more realistically, the cost were spread over five hundred aircraft, the cost of development per aircraft would be an astounding $30 million each. The viability of the new aircraft will very much be a function of Boeing's ability to contain costs within projected levels.

Notes

1. Robert M. Kane and Allan D. Vose, *Air Transportation* (Dubuque: Kendall/Hunt, 1974), p. 94.

2. Ibid., p. 94.

3. Air Transport Association of America, *Economics of Air Transport* (Washington, D.C.: ATA Press, 1972), p. 11. Reprinted with permission.

4. ATA, *Economics of Air Transport*, p. 1. Reprinted with permission.

5. Ibid., p. 1. Reprinted with permission.

6. Ibid., p. 10.

7. Ibid., p. 3. Reprinted with permission.

8. ATA, *Economics of Air Transport*, p. 11.

9. Ibid., p. 4. Reprinted with permission.

10. American Airlines, *1976 Annual Report*, p. 19.

11. Ibid., p. 18.

12. Ibid., p. 18.

13. William E. O'Connor, *Economic Regulation of the World's Airlines* (New York: Holt, Rinehart and Winston, 1971), pp. 11-12.

14. Ibid., p. 12.

15. O'Connor, *Economic Regulation of the World's Airlines*, p. 112.

16. ATA, *Economics of Air Transport*, p. 9. Reprinted with permission.

17. George Douglas and James Miller, *Economic Regulation of Domestic Air Transport*, © by the Brookings Institution, 1974, p. 28. Reprinted with permission.

18. Ibid., p. 10.

19. O'Connor, *Economic Regulation of the World's Airlines*, p. 10. Reprinted with permission.

20. Ibid., p. 11.

21. O'Connor, *Economic Regulation of the World's Airlines*, p. 11.

22. ATA, *Economics of Air Transport*, p. 8. Reprinted with permission.

23. ATA, *Economics of Air Transport*, p. 8.

24. Ibid., p. 8. Reprinted with permission.

25. Civil Aeronautics Board, Financial and Cost Section, *Operating Expenses by Functional Groupings*, July 1976 (Washington: CAB Printing Office).

26. CAB, *Operating Expenses*, July 1976.

27. Air Transport Association, *Air Transport 1976*, p. 6. Reprinted with permission.

28. American Airlines, *1976 Annual Report*, p. 19.

29. ATA, *Airline Financial Performance, 1976-1977*, p. 13.

30. Ibid., p. 14.

31. Ibid., p. 14.

32. ATA, *Air Transport 1976*, p. 6. Reprinted with permission.

33. Statistics developed from raw data on CAB *Form 41*, filed with that agency by the respective carriers.

34. James P. Woolsey, "Uncertainties Cloud U.S. Airplane Programs," *Air Transport World*, April 1977, p. 21. Reprinted with permission.

35. Ibid., p. 21. Reprinted with permission.

36. Ibid., p. 21.

37. Woolsey, "Uncertainties Cloud U.S. Airplane Programs," p. 21. Reprinted with permission.

38. H. Byrne and E. Kelliher, "The Big Buy," *Wall Street Journal*, September 25, 1978.

39. Woolsey, "Uncertainties Cloud U.S. Airplane Programs," p. 21. Reprinted with permission.

3 Estimated Capital Requirements

The task now is to assess the magnitude and timing of capital requirements for the eleven largest airlines in the United States. The first issue to be resolved is the appropriate time boundary for the study. A 1976 paper prepared by the Civil Aeronautics Board chose the period ending December 31, 1985.[1] The same period was chosen by a brokerage study on airline capital needs.[2] There is, however, a significant problem associated with using this date as a terminal point for a study: it ends just before the largest equipment needs. Aircraft acquired after 1969 would not figure into replacement estimates, and the largest planes were delivered in a major reequipment period that began at that time. The arbitrary selection of any point in time is less preferable than following the entire life of an existing fleet. This not only permits the estimation of capital needs for replacement and growth over any intermediate period, but also the penetration of underlying problems—such as clustered capacity requirements—that may appear anywhere in the fleet life cycle.

Estimates have therefore been developed for the period December 31, 1976 to December 31, 1994 (tables 3-1 through 3-12). The latter is the year in which, under the assumption of greatest aircraft longevity (eighteen years), the last plane in service on December 31, 1976 becomes obsolete. The emphasis throughout will be on the period ending December 31, 1989.

Tables 3-13 to 3-24 contain estimates of capital requirements by trunk carrier by year under twelve alternative combinations of assumptions. Appendix A lists by tail number every aircraft, both owned and held under capital lease, in the operating passenger fleets on December 31, 1976. The date of acquisition, the number of seats in each aircraft, and the year of replacement given either a sixteen or eighteen year life are presented. Table 3-25 shows the estimated cost of replacing one aircraft seat under different assumptions with respect to inflation. But before analyzing the individual carriers, a brief discussion of methodology is in order.

The components of capital needs are as follows: (1) the size of existing capacity and the timing of its obsolescence; (2) the cost per period of new equipment; and (3) additional capacity required for growth.

Various studies have chosen aircraft lives ranging from sixteen to twenty years.[3] Assuming a life longer than eighteen years would not be realistic in light of noise regulations and the need for greater operating economies. The Air Transport Association chose an eighteen-year service life, and this figure is relied upon here, although the impact of a sixteen-year life is also shown. In addressing the issue, the ATA indicated that the eighteen-year life is "believed to be

Table 3-1
Summary of Capital Requirements for American Airlines
(thousands of dollars)

Year	Replacement	Growth (5 Percent)	Growth (7 Percent)	Replacement + Midpoint of 5 Percent/ 7 Percent Growth[a]
1977- 1979	256,357	364,210	516,647	696,785.5
1980	–	237,494	351,725	294,609.5
1981	–	269,131	406,376	337,753.5
1982	237,397	305,351	469,749	624,947.0
1983	296,770	346,125	542,743	741,204.0
1984	351,316	392,678	627,177	861,243.5
1985	822,204	445,212	724,825	1,407,222.5
1986	1,101,550	504,650	837,719	1,772,734.5
1987	971,008	572,707	967,955	1,741,339.0
1988	519,871	649,133	1,118,383	1,403,629.0
1989	305,142	736,155	1,292,531	1,319,485.0
1990	1,318,214	834,870	1,493,977	2,487,137.5
1991	–	946,741	1,725,904	1,336,322.5
1992	–	1,073,412	1,994,990	1,534,201.0
1993	260,848	1,217,751	2,305,078	2,022,262.5
1994	–	1,807,612	3,090,651	2,449,131.5
Total after 1989	1,579,062	5,880,386	10,610,600	9,824,555.0
Total	6,440,677	10,703,232	18,466,430	21,025,508.0

[a]Total replacement + 5 percent growth = $17.1 billion through 1994; total replacement + 7 percent growth = $24.9 billion through 1994.

realistic, but certainly conservative when compared to the nine year average age of airplanes sold or retired in 1975."[4] This statement is somewhat misleading, since certain of the aircraft disposed of were almost new B-747's which were sold to eliminate excess capacity that was plaguing the industry, not because of obsolescence.

The unit of capacity in the airline industry is the aircraft seat. One passenger seat costs roughly the same in any given year regardless of the manufacturer chosen. The ATA estimated that the cost for the purchase of the weighted average seat ordered by the domestic trunk carriers in 1976 was $93,500. The cost per seat methodology was developed by the industry to comply with the replacement cost disclosure for *Form 10-K* filed annually with the Securities and Exchange Commission (SEC). The SEC concurred that the appropriate unit by which to quantify industry capacity is the aircraft passenger seat.

The first major issue is at what annual rate to escalate the cost of an aircraft seat. For purposes of this study, all increases in the unit cost of capacity will be termed "inflation" regardless of possible qualitative improvements such as comfort, safety, speed, or efficiency. We are concerned here with capital

Table 3-2

Summary of Capital Requirements for Braniff International Corporation
(thousands of dollars)

Year	Replacement	Growth (5 Percent)	Growth (7 Percent)	Replacement + Midpoint of 5 Percent/ 7 Percent Growth[a]
1977- 1979	–	119,655	169,812	144,733.5
1980	–	78,104	115,630	96,867.0
1981	–	88,337	133,535	110,936.0
1982	–	100,449	154,456	127,452.0
1983	–	113,773	178,350	146,061.5
1984	88,262	128,931	206,116	255,785.5
1985	401,102	146,349	238,120	593,336.5
1986	–	165,929	275,337	220,633.0
1987	95,488	188,140	318,073	348,594.5
1988	91,825	213,317	367,536	382,251.5
1989	156,640	241,825	424,910	490,007.5
Subtotal	833,317	1,584,809	2,581,875	2,916,659.0
1990	369,649	274,354	490,761	752,206.5
1991	756,325	311,131	567,392	1,195,586.5
1992	208,212	352,999	655,387	712,405
1993	314,816	399,921	757,635	893,594
1994	388,573	453,585	875,411	1,053,071
Total after 1989	2,037,575	1,791,990	3,346,586	4,606,863.0
Total	2,870,892	3,376,799	5,928,461	7,523,522.0

[a]Replacement + 5 percent growth = $6.2 billion through 1994; replacement + 7 percent growth = $8.8 billion through 1994.

requirements, and the cost of providing the service over time is the immediately relevant factor. Table 3-26 highlights the extreme nature of the inflation that has characterized aircraft prices in recen times.

A 747 delivered to United Airlines in 1972 costed $20,543,000.[5] The same aircraft ordered in 1978 would have a delivered cost of about $46,000,000. Even allowing an exaggerated three-year lead time for the delivery of aircraft UA-4723, the annual rate of inflation is 9.3 percent. A DC-10 delivered to American Airlines in 1972 had a delivered price of $14,973,000. The 1978 price of $28,000,000 represents an 8.2 percent annual rate of inflation, even assuming a two and one-half year lead time in ordering aircraft AA-114. In 1973 Delta took delivery of Aircraft No. 459, a Boeing 727-200. The cost was $6,258,935. The 1978 price of $12,000,000 exhibits a 9.5 percent annual inflation rate, even assuming a two-year delivery period.[6] Boeing's estimate for aircraft actually delivered in 1976 showed the following price change over 1975:[7] B-727-200, up 10.8 percent; B747-200B, up 13.0 percent. The similar figures for 1977 versus 1976 are: B-727-200, up 8.6 percent; B747-200B, up 7.3 percent.

Table 3-3
Summary of Capital Requirements for Continental Airlines
(thousands of dollars)

Year	Replacement	Growth (5 Percent)	Growth (7 Percent)	Replacement + Midpoint of 5 Percent/ 7 Percent Growth[a]
1977- 1979	–	94,959	134,735	114,847.0
1980	–	168,548	240,547	204,547.5
1981	–	70,202	105,922	88,062.0
1982	–	79,676	122,556	101,116.0
1983	–	90,217	160,243	25,230.0
1984	–	102,280	163,371	132,825.5
1985	–	116,069	188,963	152,516.0
1986	310,359	131,613	218,412	485,271.5
1987	52,104	149,117	252,235	252,780.0
1988	150,687	169,356	291,816	381,273.0
1989	–	191,985	336,928	264,456.0
Subtotal	513,050	1,364,022	2,215,728	2,302,925.0
1990	442,151	217,505	389,423	745,615.0
1991	446,380	246,770	449,939	794,734.5
1992	424,112	279,965	519,889	824,039.0
1993	461,500	317,238	600,919	920,578.5
1994	80,704	360,177	694,200	607,892.5
Total after 1989	1,854,847	1,421,655	2,654,370	3,892,859.5
Total	2,367,897	2,785,677	4,870,098	6,195,784.5

[a]Total replacement + 5 percent growth = $5.2 billion through 1994; total replacement + 7 percent growth = $7.2 billion through 1994.

There is little basis for assuming a rate of 6 percent as have earlier studies. The Donaldson study used a rate of 5 percent in developing its estimate for the 1976-1985 period. The ATA used 6 percent, but acknowledged the problems with this rate "A 6% annual average inflation [has been assumed] for the cost per seat of new equipment, whereas actual aircraft cost inflation has been closer to 15% annually in recent years."[8] The present study has selected an 8 percent inflation rate, which appears most reasonable in light of the past ten years and the prospects for the future. As discussed in a prior section, new aircraft technologies such as those to be embodied in the 757/767 are going to cost more per seat because of huge developmental costs, long gestation periods, and a more expensive level of technology to implement. The effect of assuming 7 percent and, as a lower boundary, 5 percent inflation are shown for purposes of sensitivity analysis. In this way the effect of the assumptions actually selected can be evaluated and this study can be adapted for policy purposes as events unfold.

Another pivotal assumption is the annual rate of growth in the demand for

Table 3-4
Summary of Capital Requirements for Delta Airlines
(thousands of dollars)

Year	Replacement	Growth (5 Percent)	Growth (7 Percent)	Replacement + Midpoint of 5 Percent/ 7 Percent Growth[a]
1977-
1979	73,760	314,818	446,712	454,525.0
1980	68,691	205,311	304,023	323,358.0
1981	—	232,725	351,286	292,005.5
1982	60,091	263,807	406,097	395,043.0
1983	64,898	299,334	469,192	449,161.0
1984	46,727	339,374	542,203	487,515.5
1985	254,567	384,842	626,513	760,244.5
1986	633,033	436,421	724,072	1,213,279.5
1987	554,612	494,879	836,933	1,220,518.0
1988	388,491	561,310	966,753	1,152,522.5
1989	91,543	636,475	1,117,582	968,571.5
Subtotal	2,236,413	4,169,296	6,791,366	7,716,744.0
1990	259,523	721,723	1,291,027	1,265,898.0
1991	1,184,612	818,314	1,492,185	2,339,861.5
1992	1,753,465	927,984	1,724,635	3,079,774.5
1993	934,070	1,052,386	1,992,684	2,456,605.0
1994	1,275,192	1,193,742	2,302,670	3,023,398.0
Total after 1989	5,406,862	4,714,149	8,803,201	12,165,537.0
Total	7,643,275	8,883,445	15,594,567	19,882,281.0

[a]Replacement + 5 percent growth = $16.5 billion through 1994; replacement + 7 percent growth = $23.2 billion through 1994.

air travel. Between 1966 and 1975 the growth was 7.1 percent.[9] In 1976 revenue passenger miles increased 11 percent as shown in table 3-27. The ATA study chose a 5 percent growth figure even though reservations were expressed. "A 5% traffic growth factor [is assumed] although the actual 1976 growth will be about 10%."[10] The 5 percent estimate for traffic growth, like the 6 percent inflation factor, make the estimates derived significantly biased downward.

In a review of aviation in the United States, the National Aeronautics and Space Administration (NASA) has indicated the following: "Energy considerations, mode competition, [and] life style change imply an annual growth of about 7% in revenue passenger miles for the next ten years."[11] The Federal Aviation Agency (FAA) takes a somewhat more conservative position, holding that domestic revenue passenger miles will increase 5.9 percent annually until 1988.[12] A reasonable yet conservative estimate is the simple average of the estimates generated for 5 percent and 7 percent growth, or approximately 6.05 percent annually. This is the rate used in the present study.

The 1977-1979 period is characterized on the margin by two offsetting

Table 3-5
Summary of Capital Requirements for Eastern Airlines
(thousands of dollars)

Year	Replacement	Growth (5 Percent)	Growth (7 Percent)	Replacement + Midpoint of 5 Percent/ 7 Percent Growth[a]
1977-				
1979	133,751	347,820	493,482	554,402.0
1980	–	226,681	335,824	281,252.5
1981	29,400	257,041	388,241	352,041.0
1982	252,828	291,701	448,531	622,944.0
1983	218,693	331,581	519,386	644,176.5
1984	238,133	374,853	598,968	725,043.5
1985	407,083	425,214	692,304	965,842.0
1986	1,039,983	482,243	799,769	1,680,989.0
1987	403,315	546,546	924,572	1,138,874.0
1988	124,317	620,173	1,068,232	968,519.5
1989	360,322	703,098	1,234,299	1,329,020.5
Subtotal	3,207,825	4,606,951	7,503,068	9,263,104.5
1990	884,302	797,245	1,426,418	1,996,133.5
1991	1,891,702	904,031	1,648,788	3,168,111.5
1992	254,659	1,025,364	1,904,979	1,719,330.5
1993	630,670	998,682	1,942,223	2,101,122.5
1994	583,981	561,816	1,299,878	1,514,828.0
Total after 1989	4,245,314	4,287,138	8,222,286	10,500,026.0
Total	7,453,139	8,894,089	15,725,894	19,763,130.5

[a]Total replacement + 5 percent growth = $16.3 billion through 1994; total replacement + 7 percent growth = $15.7 billion through 1994.

factors. One is the ability to increase utilization through slightly higher load factors than were achieved in 1976. The other factor is growth higher than the 6 percent assumed for the longer period. If 1977 growth rate of 7.5 percent continues through 1979, the airlines in question will have an average load factor of slightly over 60 percent—the probable practical maximum in view of the varying markets served by the different carriers and the industry's seasonal trends. The estimates that follow, therefore, assume that the 1976 load factor of 55.8 percent[13] can be raised to 60 percent by 1980, at which point load factors will become level. Traffic growth will average approximately 6 percent thereafter.

American Airlines is the second largest carrier in this study, flying about one-half as many revenue passenger miles as the industry giant, United Airlines. In a prospectus filed with its Form 10-K for 1976, the company addresses the impact of noise control legislation. "The regulations require modification or replacement of aircraft that do not meet present FAA noise control standards for new aircraft with compliance required over a four year period beginning in 1981."

Table 3-6
Summary of Capital Requirements for National Airlines
(thousands of dollars)

Year	Replacement	Growth (5 Percent)	Growth (7 Percent)	Replacement + Midpoint of 5 Percent/ 7 Percent Growth[a]
1977-				
1979	–	100,641	142,712	121,676.5
1980	–	65,511	97,185	81,348.0
1981	–	74,324	112,241	93,282.5
1982	63,504	84,424	129,678	170,355.0
1983	124,669	95,505	149,827	247,335.0
1984	55,553	108,510	173,235	196,425.5
1985	76,258	122,985	200,177	237,839.0
1986	576,512	139,284	231,332	761,820.0
1987	–	158,274	267,496	212,885.0
1988	–	179,177	308,909	244,043.0
1989	205,971	203,428	357,016	486,193.0
Subtotal	1,102,467	1,332,063	2,169,808	2,853,402.5
1990	444,897	230,413	412,492	766,349.5
1991	169,654	261,599	476,633	538,770.0
1992	–	296,622	550,961	423,791.5
1993	384,699	335,919	636,551	870,934.0
1994	–	381,474	735,674	558,574.0
Total after 1989	999,250	1,506,027	2,812,311	3,158,419.0
Total	2,101,717	2,838,090	4,982,119	6,011,821.5

[a]Total replacement + 5 percent growth = $4.9 billion through 1994; total replacement + 7 percent growth = $7.1 billion through 1994.

The Company maintains that it can retrofit newer aircraft—DC-10's, B-747's, and B-727-200's—to comply with the regulations for relatively little cost. All of the B-707 aircraft, however, "must be brought into compliance or replaced by 1985."[14] The cost of this reequipping is said to be substantial. "American estimates that the cost of modifying or replacing its owned and leased Boeing 707 aircraft would be very substantial, and could have a material adverse effect on American."[15] In its 1977 annual report, American indicates that "replacement is the obvious course to follow." The eighteen-year life employed in this study has American's last 707 being replaced in 1985—the year when noise regulations would mandate it.

American's statement of intention to replace its 707 fleet appears to be confirmed by recent purchases. In its 1976 *10-K* and 1977 annual report, the company discloses a total purchase of twenty-one B-727's and six DC-10's to be delivered before 1980. This should provide over four thousand of the 6,400 new seats this study estimates that American will require by 1980. As has been observed, "the average age of American's fleet is among the highest in the industry," and one may expect a period of necessary catch-up in aircraft

Table 3-7
Summary of Capital Requirements for Northwest Airlines
(thousands of dollars)

Year	Replacement	Growth (5 Percent)	Growth (7 Percent)	Replacement + Midpoint of 5 Percent/ 7 Percent Growth[a]
1977-				
1979	–	222,810	316,130	269,470.0
1980	–	136,238	215,233	175,735.5
1981	–	164,721	248,661	206,691.0
1982	41,396	186,802	287,399	278,496.5
1983	163,929	211,841	332,023	435,861.0
1984	160,948	240,210	383,851	472,978.5
1985	104,294	272,324	443,530	462,221.0
1986	510,706	308,846	512,522	921,390.0
1987	418,575	350,339	592,328	889,908.5
1988	868,807	397,438	684,215	1,409,633.5
1989	469,156	450,339	791,080	1,089,865.5
Subtotal	2,737,811	2,941,908	4,806,972	6,612,251.0
1990	–	510,808	913,962	712,385.0
1991	1,049,957	579,256	1,056,185	1,867,677.5
1992	529,179	656,988	1,220,442	1,467,894.0
1993	354,255	744,835	1,410,446	1,431,895.5
1994	275,737	844,773	1,630,139	1,513,193.0
Total after 1989	2,209,138	3,336,660	6,231,174	6,993,045.0
Total	4,946,939	6,278,568	11,038,146	13,605,296.0

[a]Replacement + 5 percent growth = $11.2 billion through 1994; replacement + 7 percent growth = $16.0 billion through 1994.

replacement. As that same Donaldson study points out, United and TWA—American's principal competitors—are confronted with similar difficulties, and all may benefit financially in the short run from the higher load factors that tight capacity is bringing about. American's capital requirements for the period ending in 1989 are estimated to be $4.86 billion for replacement and $6.34 billion for expansion.

Braniff has a relatively modern fleet, but will need major equipment changes in the late 1980s and early 1990s. The present study has five of the seven DC-8-62's in Braniff's fleet becoming obsolete in 1985 and the remaining two in 1987. Under FAA noise regulations, it is possible that these two aircraft would also have to be phased out in 1985.

On December 31, 1976 Braniff had on order eighteen B-727 aircraft at a contracted cost of $204,482,000. Since there are no immediate replacement needs (estimated here to begin in 1984), these are strictly to accommodate growth. The purchase is consistent with the study's growth assumptions. The new aircraft will furnish approximately 2,340 new seats. For the period ending in 1980, a need of 2,086 has been projected.

Table 3-8

Summary of Capital Requirements for Pan American World Airways

(thousands of dollars)

Year	Replacement	Growth (5 Percent)	Growth (7 Percent)	Replacement + Midpoint of 5 Percent/ 7 Percent Growth[a]
1977-1979	–	280,179	397,539	338,859.0
1980	–	182,668	270,694	226,681.0
1981	–	207,035	312,681	259,858.0
1982	83,237	234,875	361,289	381,319.0
1983	299,654	266,485	417,594	641,693.5
1984	316,877	301,993	482,496	709,121.5
1985	702,770	342,414	557,731	1,152,842.5
1986	452,974	390,397	644,337	970,341.0
1987	565,513	440,594	744,715	1,158,167.5
1988	1,789,883	499,388	860,566	2,469,860.0
1989	552,307	566,293	994,509	1,332,708.0
Subtotal	4,763,215	3,712,321	6,044,151	9,641,451.0
1990	–	642,355	1,149,044	895,699.5
1991	107,368	728,445	1,346,166	1,144,673.5
1992	–	825,800	1,534,682	1,180,241.0
1993	–	936,838	1,773,350	1,355,094.0
1994	676,267	1,062,224	2,049,349	2,323,053.5
Total after 1989	783,635	4,195,662	7,852,591	6,807,761.5
Total	5,546,850	7,907,983	13,896,742	16,449,212.5

[a]Total replacement + 5 percent growth = $13.5 billion through 1994; total replacement + 7 percent growth = $19.4 billion through 1994.

Braniff's requirements are estimated to be $833.3 million for replacement and $2.08 billion for growth for the period ending December 31, 1989.

In discussing Continental Airlines, one is tempted to anticipate the next chapter, which will examine the financial characteristics of each carrier. Whereas United and American are generally believed to have stronger balance sheets but older fleets than Continental, closer scrutiny indicates that financial position is similar with respect to leverage. Continental's aircraft replacement needs before 1990 are minimal—approximately $513 million. The real issue is whether or not the funds for expansion can be acquired. These are estimated to be $3.83 billion for that same period. In its 1976 annual report, the company correctly indicated with respect to federal noise standards: "[Your] airline is less affected by this ruling than those of our competitors." The company also speaks of its wise decision to opt for replacement of forty-four planes in the 1970-1976 period:

> The current modern fleet . . . was acquired at a cost of approximately $630 million. It would cost slightly over $1 billion to replace these assets in today's market. . . . [T]he Company could not undertake such

Table 3-9
Summary of Capital Requirements for Trans World Airlines
(thousands of dollars)

Year	Replacement	Growth (5 Percent)	Growth (7 Percent)	Replacement + Midpoint of 5 Percent/ 7 Percent Growth[a]
1977- 1979	176,478	374,263	530,962	629,090.5
1980	226,172	243,981	361,393	528,859.0
1981	—	276,687	417,779	347,233.0
1982	220,779	313,661	482,657	618,938.0
1983	190,689	355,740	557,806	647,462.0
1984	575,085	403,408	644,483	1,099,030.5
1985	529,134	457,548	744,824	1,130,320.0
1986	599,928	518,780	860,933	1,289,784.5
1987	701,114	588,403	994,552	1,492,591.5
1988	874,928	667,263	1,149,463	1,783,291.0
1989	470,682	756,497	1,328,384	1,513,122.5
Subtotal	4,564,989	4,956,231	8,073,236	11,079,722.5
1990	563,262	857,938	1,535,171	1,759,816.5
1991	606,543	972,841	1,773,953	1,979,940.0
1992	1,135,876	1,103,523	2,049,766	2,712,520.5
1993	397,845	1,250,962	2,368,733	2,207,692.5
1994	135,627	1,418,665	2,737,572	2,213,745.5
Total after 1989	2,839,153	5,603,929	10,465,195	10,873,715.0
Total	7,404,142	10,560,160	18,538,431	21,953,437.5

[a]Total replacement + 5 percent growth through 1994 = $18.0 billion; total replacement + 7 percent growth through 1994 = $25.9 billion.

a re-equipping program today, nor can most of the major airlines, due to the enormous increase in financing capital required, together with interest cost thereon.[16]

Delta is by all criteria one of the most successful airlines in the industry. In its Form 10-K for the year ending June 30, 1977,[17] Delta indicates that "At June 30, 1977, the Company had outstanding purchase commitments for the acquisition of thirty-six Boeing 727-200 aircraft and nine Lockheed L-1011 aircraft."[18] This will yield approximately 7,164 seats, assuming continuity in the company's choice of seating configuration: $(9 \times 256) + (36 \times 135)$. These aircraft will be delivered over the period ending in February 1979, and confirm the range of the estimate that the company will require over 6,700 seats by the end of 1980. Delta will require $2.24 billion for replacement and $5.48 billion for capacity expansion by the end of 1989.

It has been suggested that Delta will expand its capacity more than strictly necessary to win market share from its troubled competitor, Eastern Airlines.

Table 3-10
Summary of Capital Requirements for United Airlines
(thousands of dollars)

Year	Replacement	Growth (5 Percent)	Growth (7 Percent)	Replacement + Midpoint of 5 Percent/ 7 Percent Growth[a]
1977-				
1979	499,601	562,433	797,919	1,179,777.0
1980	–	366,608	543,042	454,825.0
1981	39,566	415,718	627,698	561,274.0
1982	313,364	471,381	725,395	911,752.0
1983	398,735	505,196	808,696	1,055,681.0
1984	688,095	606,236	968,628	1,475,527.0
1985	881,640	687,444	1,119,198	1,784,961.0
1986	2,004,672	779,785	1,293,519	3,041,324.0
1987	1,312,626	884,023	1,494,881	3,502,078.0
1988	724,712	1,002,542	1,727,254	2,089,610.0
1989	568,581	1,136,908	1,996,136	2,135,103.0
Subtotal	7,431,592	7,418,274	12,102,366	17,191,912.0
1990	1,051,825	1,289,379	2,306,875	2,849,952.0
1991	764,630	1,461,931	2,665,526	2,828,358.5
1992	542,632	1,658,008	3,080,575	2,911,923.5
1993	587,043	1,879,903	3,861,184	3,456,586.5
1994	284,705	2,132,295	4,113,644	3,407,674.5
Total after 1989	3,229,835	8,421,516	16,027,804	15,454,495.0
Total	10,661,427	15,839,790	28,130,170	32,646,407.0

[a]Total replacement + 5 percent growth = $26.5 billion through 1994; total replacement + 7 percent growth = $38.5 billion through 1994.

Eastern has and will encounter capacity shortages due to financing difficulties and equipment inadequacies. Delta will be anxious to exploit this opportunity.

While Eastern's financial difficulties will be more thoroughly explored later in this study, the key issue to be addressed here is the problem of Eastern's fleet. "Eastern Airlines is about to gamble its future," opened a recent article in the *Wall Street Journal.*[19] The article was describing Eastern's prospective purchase of twenty-five European Airbus A300 jets. Eastern, as the article indicates, "has been flying one of the most inefficient fleets of airplanes in the U.S."[20] Costs in 1976 per ton mile were forty cents, as opposed to thirty-four for Delta and twenty-eight for National. The article further notes that Eastern has too many small planes equipped to seat one hundred passengers, such as the DC-9 and early model 727's and too many very large planes (L-1011's). "Eastern is sometimes forced to put two little planes on the route—a costly measure. Or it is forced to employ a huge Lockheed—also a costly measure because of the plane's overcapacity." In many cases Eastern cannot double capacity by doubling the number of small planes because of a lack of gates. This constraint is operative in Atlanta, for example.

Table 3-11
Summary of Capital Requirements for Western Airlines
(thousands of dollars)

Year	Replacement	Growth (5 Percent)	Growth (7 Percent)	Replacement + Midpoint of 5 Percent/ 7 Percent Growth[a]
1977-				
1979	27,974	107,741	152,870	158,279.5
1980	48,847	70,218	104,055	135,983.5
1981	35,170	79,681	120,209	135,115.0
1982	–	90,359	139,026	114,692.5
1983	61,533	102,396	160,564	193,013.0
1984	88,608	116,124	185,522	239,431.0
1985	95,696	131,770	214,570	268,866.0
1986	404,729	149,377	247,884	603,359.5
1987	353,827	169,392	286,244	581,645.0
1988	–	191,891	331,041	261,466.0
1989	–	217,922	382,445	300,183.5
Subtotal	1,116,384	1,426,871	2,324,430	2,992,034.5
1990	167,523	247,165	442,151	512,181.0
1991	301,344	279,988	510,445	696,560.5
1992	354,921	317,764	590,361	808,983.5
1993	214,490	360,136	671,493	730,304.5
1994	94,902	400,902	788,355	689,530.5
Total after 1989	1,133,180	1,605,955	3,002,805	3,437,560.0
Total	2,249,564	3,032,826	5,327,235	6,429,594.5

[a]Total replacement + 5 percent growth = $5.3 billion through 1994; total replacement + 7 percent growth = $7.6 billion through 1994.

Without exploring the possible commercial merits of the Airbus for Eastern, we can say that the twenty-five aircraft, each of which has 230 seats, will give Eastern 5,750 seats. Based on the assumptions discussed previously, Eastern will require 1,224 seats for capacity replacement and 3,850 to meet growing demand, for a total of 5,074 before 1980. Eastern needs these planes or a suitable alternative in the immediate future.

Eastern's capital requirements for the period ending in 1989 are estimated to be $3.21 billion for capacity replacement and $6.06 billion for growth.

For Eastern—heavily leveraged and flying an undesirable fleet—the failure to acquire needed funds will probably mean the failure to survive, at least as a separate entity. One study for the period ending in 1985 characterized National Airlines' capacity replacement needs over this period as "relatively light."[21] In 1986 alone, however, 32 percent of its year-end 1976 fleet must be replaced. This typifies the need to study the entire aircraft replacement cycle, even when primary consideration is being given to some shorter time span. In its 1976 Form 10-K the company indicates that "the fleet now consists of fifteen DC-10's

Table 3-12
Summary of Capital Requirements through 1989
(thousands of dollars)

Airline	Replacement	Growth	Total
American	4,861,615	6,339,338.0	11,200,953.0
Braniff	833,317	2,083,342.0	2,916,659.0
Continental	513,050	1,789,875.0	2,302,925.0
Delta	2,236,413	5,480,331.0	7,716,744.0
Eastern	3,207,825	6,055,279.5	9,263,104.5
National	1,102,467	1,750,935.5	2,853,402.5
Northwest	2,737,811	3,874,440.0	6,612,251.0
Pan American	4,763,215	4,878,236.0	9,641,451.0
Trans World	4,564,989	6,514,733.5	11,079,722.5
United	7,431,592	9,760,320.0	17,191,912.0
Western	1,116,384	1,875,650.5	2,992,034.5
Total	33,368,678	50,402,480	83,771,158

[a]This represents the forecasted capital requirement for the period in question: $83.8 billion for the years 1977-1989.

including four intercontinental models and 38 727's of which 13 are standard and 25 long-body models. Management correctly characterizes National's fleet as "modern and one of the most efficient in the industry."[22]

National also poses a threat to Eastern, since it has the wherewithal to finance additional capacity if circumstances dictate. One possible constraint on growth has been the company's perennial labor problems. Shut down in 1975 by one strike, the company was again closed down for one hundred twenty-six days in 1976 by another strike. National's capital needs for the period ending in 1989 are estimated to be $1.10 billion for replacement and $1.75 billion for expansion.

Northwest, like Delta, is a financially strong airline. Capital required for aircraft replacement will approximate $2.74 billion for the period ending December 31, 1989, while funds for expansion are estimated at $3.87 billion. In its 1976 Form 10-K, Northwest indicates that nine Boeing 727's are to be delivered in the next year. "The 727's on order will increase to 40 the fleet of this type aircraft."[23] These aircraft on order at the end of 1976 will provide 1,152 of the 2,466 seats envisioned as required for growth by 1980. This most successful and progressive company is well ahead of the timetable set in this study for the disposal of older aircraft. While the study assumes phase out in 1982, Northwest has already begun modernization in 1976. "The Company also has firm contracts for the sale and delivery . . . of five Boeing 727-100's."[24]

Northwest will not be pressured by noise regulations, since its subject aircraft will all have been retired by the 1985 deadline. All indications are that Northwest—whose annual traffic growth has been over 8 percent for the past eight years—will continue to expand rapidly.

Table 3-13
Capital Requirements Assuming 8 Percent Inflation, 18-Year Aircraft Life, 7 Percent Growth
(thousands of dollars)

Year	American	Braniff	Continental	Delta	Eastern	National	Northwest	Pan American	Trans World	United	Western	Total
1977–1979	773,004	169,812	134,735	520,472	627,233	142,712	316,130	397,539	707,440	1,297,519	180,844	5,267,440
1980	351,725	115,630	240,547	372,714	335,824	97,185	215,233	270,694	587,565	543,042	152,902	3,283,061
1981	406,376	133,535	105,922	351,286	417,641	112,241	248,661	312,681	417,779	667,264	155,379	3,328,765
1982	707,146	154,456	122,556	466,188	701,359	193,182	328,795	444,526	703,436	1,038,759	139,026	4,999,439
1983	839,513	178,350	160,243	534,090	738,079	274,496	495,952	717,248	748,495	1,207,431	222,097	6,115,994
1984	978,493	294,378	163,371	588,930	837,101	228,788	544,799	799,373	1,219,568	1,656,723	274,130	7,585,654
1985	1,547,029	639,222	188,963	881,080	1,099,387	276,435	547,824	1,260,501	1,273,958	2,000,839	310,266	10,025,504
1986	1,939,269	275,337	528,671	1,357,105	1,839,752	807,844	1,023,228	1,097,311	1,460,861	3,298,191	652,613	14,280,182
1987	1,938,963	413,561	304,339	1,391,545	1,327,887	267,496	1,010,903	1,310,228	1,695,666	2,807,507	640,071	13,108,166
1988	1,638,254	459,361	442,503	1,355,244	1,192,549	308,909	1,553,022	2,650,449	2,024,391	2,451,966	331,041	14,407,689
1989	1,597,673	581,550	336,928	1,209,125	1,594,621	562,987	1,260,236	1,546,816	1,799,066	2,564,719	382,445	13,436,166
1990	2,812,191	860,410	831,574	1,550,550	2,310,720	857,389	913,962	1,149,044	2,098,433	3,358,700	609,674	17,352,647
1991	1,725,904	1,323,717	896,319	2,676,797	3,540,490	646,287	2,106,142	1,453,534	2,380,496	3,430,156	811,789	20,991,631
1992	1,994,990	863,599	944,001	3,478,100	2,159,638	550,961	1,749,621	1,534,682	3,185,642	3,623,207	945,282	21,029,723
1993	2,565,926	1,072,451	1,062,419	2,926,754	2,572,893	1,021,250	1,764,701	1,773,350	2,766,578	4,145,889	885,983	22,558,194
1994	3,090,651	1,263,984	774,904	3,577,862	1,883,859	735,674	1,905,876	2,725,616	2,873,199	4,398,344	883,257	24,113,226
Total	24,907,107	8,799,353	7,237,995	23,237,842	23,179,033	7,083,836	15,985,085	19,443,592	25,942,573	38,490,256	7,576,799	201,883,471

Total through 1989: $95.8 billion.

Table 3-14
Capital Requirements Assuming 8 Percent Inflation, 18-Year Aircraft Life, 5 Percent Growth
(thousands of dollars)

Year	American	Braniff	Continental	Delta	Eastern	National	Northwest	Pan American	Trans World	United	Western	Total
1977-1979	620,567	119,655	94,959	388,578	481,571	100,641	222,810	280,179	550,741	1,062,034	135,715	4,057,450
1980	237,494	78,104	168,548	274,002	226,681	65,511	136,238	182,668	470,153	366,608	119,065	2,325,072
1981	269,131	88,337	70,202	232,725	286,441	74,324	164,721	207,035	276,687	455,284	114,851	2,239,738
1982	542,748	100,449	79,676	323,898	544,529	147,928	228,198	318,112	534,440	784,745	90,359	3,695,082
1983	642,895	113,773	90,217	364,232	550,274	220,174	375,770	566,139	546,429	903,931	163,929	4,537,763
1984	743,994	217,193	102,280	386,101	612,986	164,063	401,158	618,870	978,493	1,294,331	204,732	5,724,201
1985	1,267,416	547,451	116,069	639,409	832,297	199,243	376,618	1,045,184	986,682	1,569,084	227,466	7,806,919
1986	1,606,200	165,929	441,872	1,069,454	1,522,226	715,796	819,552	843,371	1,118,708	2,784,457	554,106	11,641,671
1987	1,543,715	283,628	201,221	1,049,491	949,861	158,274	768,914	1,006,107	1,289,517	2,196,649	523,219	9,970,596
1988	1,169,004	305,142	320,043	949,801	744,490	179,177	1,266,245	2,289,271	1,542,191	1,727,254	191,891	10,684,509
1989	1,041,297	398,465	191,985	728,018	1,063,420	409,399	919,495	1,118,600	1,227,179	1,705,489	217,922	9,021,269
1990	2,153,084	644,003	659,656	981,246	1,681,547	675,310	510,808	642,355	1,421,200	2,341,204	414,688	12,125,101
1991	946,741	1,067,456	693,150	2,002,926	2,795,733	431,253	1,629,213	835,813	1,579,384	2,226,561	581,332	14,789,562
1992	1,073,412	561,211	704,077	2,681,449	1,280,023	296,622	1,186,167	825,800	2,239,399	2,200,640	672,685	13,721,485
1993	1,478,599	714,737	778,738	1,986,456	1,629,352	720,618	1,099,090	936,838	1,648,807	2,465,946	574,626	14,033,807
1994	1,807,612	842,158	440,881	2,468,934	1,145,797	381,474	1,120,510	1,738,491	1,554,292	2,417,000	495,804	14,412,953
Total	17,143,909	6,247,691	5,153,574	16,526,720	16,347,728	4,939,807	11,225,507	13,454,833	17,964,302	26,501,217	5,282,390	140,787,178

Total through 1989: $71.7 billion.

Table 3-15
Capital Requirements Assuming 8 Percent Inflation, 16-Year Aircraft Life, 7 Percent Growth
(thousands of dollars)

Year	American	Braniff	Continental	Delta	Eastern	National	Northwest	Pan American	Trans World	United	Western	Total
1977-1979	773,004	169,812	134,735	579,480	650,617	142,712	316,130	397,539	901,729	1,328,990	250,777	5,645,525
1980	555,254	115,630	240,547	355,541	552,583	151,630	250,723	342,057	550,675	811,701	104,055	4,030,396
1981	660,807	133,535	105,922	407,887	576,592	219,124	389,203	569,586	581,263	944,226	172,964	4,761,109
1982	770,946	230,127	122,556	446,158	852,963	177,306	425,385	632,959	975,701	1,315,327	214,992	6,164,420
1983	1,247,652	522,232	141,495	687,442	867,395	215,206	421,439	1,020,107	1,011,454	1,594,097	242,608	7,971,127
1984	1,571,576	206,117	429,367	1,084,926	1,490,583	667,500	821,698	870,848	1,158,823	2,687,307	532,512	11,521,257
1985	1,557,309	319,985	233,634	1,102,004	1,038,081	200,177	802,392	1,042,567	1,345,917	2,244,566	517,919	10,404,551
1986	1,283,426	354,062	347,603	1,057,141	906,351	231,332	1,257,386	2,178,877	1,611,045	1,914,844	247,884	11,389,951
1987	1,229,565	452,367	252,235	915,416	1,233,489	444,082	994,552	1,218,229	1,398,085	1,982,347	286,245	10,406,612
1988	2,248,538	684,450	670,937	1,189,253	1,826,378	690,336	684,215	860,566	1,632,368	2,929,024	174,665	13,290,730
1989	1,292,531	1,073,337	719,627	2,133,197	2,856,129	502,467	1,691,250	1,086,560	1,848,398	2,651,684	640,798	16,494,978
1990	1,493,976	669,268	753,030	2,794,340	1,644,747	857,389	1,367,647	1,149,044	2,509,001	2,772,095	746,439	16,756,976
1991	1,949,539	837,296	845,601	2,292,998	2,189,486	806,450	1,359,902	1,328,166	2,115,040	3,167,963	694,336	17,586,777
1992	2,361,123	988,526	589,090	2,817,908	2,405,648	550,961	1,456,843	2,114,472	2,166,044	3,324,664	671,724	19,447,003
1993	2,305,078	757,635	600,919	1,992,684	1,999,916	636,552	1,410,446	1,773,350	2,368,733	3,559,846	681,871	18,087,030
1994	2,663,594	875,410	694,201	2,302,669	1,532,154	735,675	1,630,139	2,049,350	2,737,572	4,113,644	788,355	20,122,763
Total	23,963,918	8,389,789	6,881,499	22,159,044	22,623,112	7,228,899	15,279,350	18,634,277	24,911,848	37,042,325	6,968,144	194,082,205

Total through 1989: $102.1 billion.

Table 3-16
Capital Requirements Assuming 8 Percent Inflation, 16-Year Aircraft Life, 5 Percent Growth
(thousands of dollars)

Year	American	Braniff	Continental	Delta	Eastern	National	Northwest	Pan American	Trans World	United	Western	Total
1977– 1979	620,567	119,655	94,959	447,586	504,955	100,641	228,810	280,179	745,030	1,093,505	205,648	4,435,535
1980	441,023	78,104	168,548	256,829	443,440	199,955	171,728	254,030	433,264	635,267	70,218	3,072,406
1981	523,563	88,337	70,202	288,365	445,392	181,207	305,263	463,939	440,172	729,498	132,436	3,668,374
1982	605,362	176,119	79,676	303,868	495,863	132,052	324,788	506,545	806,704	1,061,312	166,326	4,658,615
1983	1,051,034	457,654	90,217	517,585	679,590	160,884	301,257	868,998	809,387	1,290,597	184,439	6,411,642
1984	1,377,077	128,931	368,276	882,097	1,266,468	602,775	678,057	690,344	917,748	2,324,915	463,114	9,699,802
1985	1,277,696	228,213	160,740	860,333	770,991	122,985	631,185	827,250	1,058,641	1,812,811	435,119	8,185,964
1986	950,357	244,654	260,803	769,490	588,826	139,283	1,053,709	1,922,918	1,268,892	1,401,110	149,376	8,749,418
1987	834,317	322,434	149,117	573,361	855,463	334,860	752,564	914,108	991,936	1,371,488	169,392	7,269,040
1988	1,779,288	530,231	548,477	783,810	1,378,318	560,604	397,438	499,387	1,150,168	1,904,312	335,515	9,867,548
1989	736,155	890,252	574,684	1,652,090	2,324,928	348,879	1,350,508	658,344	1,276,511	1,792,455	476,276	12,081,082
1990	834,869	452,862	581,113	2,225,036	1,015,574	230,413	964,494	642,355	1,831,769	1,754,598	551,453	11,084,336
1991	1,170,376	581,035	642,431	1,619,128	1,444,729	591,416	882,972	728,455	1,313,929	1,964,369	463,879	11,402,709
1992	1,439,545	686,136	349,155	2,021,257	1,526,033	296,622	893,389	1,405,590	1,219,801	1,902,096	399,126	12,138,752
1993	1,217,751	399,921	317,238	1,052,386	1,056,376	335,919	744,835	936,838	1,250,962	1,879,903	367,055	9,559,184
1994	1,380,555	251,825	360,177	1,193,741	794,092	381,474	844,773	1,062,224	1,418,666	2,132,295	408,375	10,228,197
Total	16,239,335	5,636,365	4,815,813	15,446,962	15,591,038	4,639,969	10,519,770	12,661,494	16,933,580	25,050,531	4,977,375	132,512,604

Total through 1989: $78.1 billion.

Table 3-17
Capital Requirements Assuming 7 Percent Inflation, 18-Year Aircraft Life, 7 Percent Growth
(thousands of dollars)

Year	American	Braniff	Continental	Delta	Eastern	National	Northwest	Pan American	Trans World	United	Western	Total
1977-1979	758,418	166,607	132,192	510,651	615,397	140,019	310,164	390,037	694,090	1,273,035	252,523	5,243,138
1980	338,876	208,862	231,759	359,098	323,556	93,635	207,370	260,806	566,100	523,204	147,316	3,260,582
1981	387,909	127,467	101,108	335,322	398,683	107,141	237,362	298,472	398,794	638,156	148,318	3,178,732
1982	668,756	146,071	115,903	440,879	663,283	182,694	310,945	420,393	665,248	982,366	131,478	4,728,016
1983	735,126	167,107	132,575	500,420	691,549	257,192	464,686	672,031	701,309	1,131,312	208,095	5,661,402
1984	908,315	273,266	151,654	546,692	776,629	212,379	505,726	742,042	1,132,101	1,537,902	254,470	7,041,176
1985	1,422,783	587,884	173,787	810,318	1,011,092	254,234	503,827	1,159,267	1,171,643	1,840,147	285,347	9,220,329
1986	1,767,006	250,879	481,710	1,236,555	1,676,329	736,084	932,336	999,838	1,331,094	3,005,216	594,642	13,011,689
1987	1,750,375	373,337	274,738	1,256,200	1,198,733	241,479	912,580	1,182,792	1,530,742		577,817	
1988	1,465,216	410,842	395,680	1,212,098	1,066,588	276,281	1,388,986	2,370,499	1,810,567	2,192,980	296,075	12,885,812
1989	1,415,692	515,309	298,550	1,071,401	1,412,988	498,861	1,116,691	1,370,628	1,594,146	2,272,588	338,883	11,905,737
1990	2,468,792	755,344	730,030	1,361,211	2,028,557	362,122	802,358	1,008,733	1,842,192	2,948,567	535,226	11,843,132
1991	1,501,122	1,151,316	779,582	2,328,170	3,079,376	562,144	1,831,838	1,248,570	2,070,459	2,983,411	706,061	18,242,149
1992	1,719,096	744,169	813,452	2,997,101	1,860,974	474,766	1,507,659	1,322,445	2,745,089	3,122,141	814,556	18,121,448
1993	2,190,604	915,582	907,017	2,498,653	2,417,727	871,870	1,506,575	1,513,959	2,361,906	3,539,462	756,389	19,479,744
1994	2,614,151	1,069,109	655,434	3,026,246	2,645,753	622,251	1,612,038	2,305,395	2,430,225	3,720,235	747,081	21,447,918
Total	22,112,237	7,863,151	6,375,171	20,491,015	21,867,214	5,893,152	14,151,141	17,265,907	23,045,705	35,245,164	6,794,282	180,104,139

Total through 1989: $88.0 billion.

Table 3-18
Capital Requirements Assuming 7 Percent Inflation, 18-Year Aircraft Life, 5 Percent Growth
(thousands of dollars)

Year	American	Braniff	Continental	Delta	Eastern	National	Northwest	Pan American	Trans World	United	Western	Total
1977– 1979	608,857	117,397	93,167	381,246	472,483	98,742	218,605	274,892	540,348	1,041,993	212,024	4,059,754
1980	228,818	75,251	162,391	263,992	218,400	63,118	131,261	175,995	452,978	353,215	114,715	2,240,134
1981	256,901	84,322	67,012	222,149	273,425	70,946	157,236	197,626	264,114	435,423	109,632	2,138,786
1982	513,283	94,995	75,351	306,314	514,967	139,897	215,809	300,842	505,425	742,142	85,454	3,494,479
1983	562,956	106,600	84,529	341,270	515,584	206,294	352,081	530,448	511,981	846,945	153,594	4,212,282
1984	690,634	201,616	94,944	358,410	568,704	152,296	372,387	574,484	908,315	1,201,501	190,049	5,313,340
1985	1,165,627	503,483	106,747	588,056	765,453	183,241	346,370	961,242	907,439	1,443,067	209,197	7,179,922
1986	1,463,523	151,190	402,621	974,456	1,387,009	652,212	746,752	766,616	1,019,335	2,537,117	504,885	10,605,716
1987	1,393,569	256,042	181,650	947,414	857,475	142,880	694,128	908,250	1,164,096	1,982,997	472,330	9,000,831
1988	1,045,530	272,912	286,178	849,480	665,854	160,251	1,132,499	2,047,469	1,379,299	1,554,815	171,623	9,565,910
1989	922,689	353,078	170,117	645,094	942,292	362,767	814,761	991,187	1,087,399	1,511,228	193,100	7,993,712
1990	1,890,169	565,363	579,105	861,425	1,476,212	592,848	448,433	563,917	1,247,656	2,055,318	364,050	10,644,496
1991	823,437	928,430	602,874	1,742,065	2,431,616	375,087	1,417,024	726,957	1,373,685	1,936,573	505,619	12,863,367
1992	924,966	483,599	606,707	2,310,622	1,103,004	255,601	1,022,128	711,598	1,929,705	1,896,305	579,657	11,823,892
1993	1,262,322	610,191	664,831	1,695,894	1,531,089	615,212	938,324	799,805	1,407,633	2,105,248	490,575	12,121,124
1994	1,528,924	712,318	372,908	2,088,287	1,609,194	322,661	947,756	1,470,460	1,314,660	2,044,359	419,364	12,830,891
Total	15,282,205	5,516,787	4,551,132	14,576,174	15,332,761	4,394,053	9,955,554	12,001,788	16,014,068	23,688,246	4,775,868	126,088,636

Total through 1989: $65.8 billion.

Table 3-19
Capital Requirements Assuming 7 Percent Inflation, 16-Year Aircraft Life, 7 Percent Growth
(thousands of dollars)

Year	American	Braniff	Continental	Delta	Eastern	National	Northwest	Pan American	Trans World	United	Western	Total
1977–1979	758,418	166,607	132,192	568,545	638,341	140,019	310,164	390,037	884,713	1,303,912	391,784	5,684,732
1980	534,970	208,862	231,759	342,552	532,396	146,090	241,564	329,561	530,558	782,049	100,253	3,980,614
1981	630,779	127,467	101,108	389,352	550,390	209,167	371,517	543,702	554,849	903,037	165,104	4,546,472
1982	729,092	217,633	115,903	421,936	617,259	167,680	402,292	598,597	922,731	1,243,919	203,321	5,640,363
1983	1,092,516	489,310	132,575	644,105	812,713	201,639	394,871	955,798	947,690	1,493,603	227,313	7,392,133
1984	1,458,863	191,334	398,573	1,007,115	1,382,903	619,627	762,766	808,391	1,075,712	2,494,573	494,320	10,694,177
1985	1,432,237	294,286	214,870	1,013,499	954,710	184,101	737,950	958,836	1,237,823	2,064,299	476,324	9,568,935
1986	1,169,421	322,611	316,726	963,236	825,841	210,783	1,145,694	1,985,330	1,467,937	1,744,750	225,865	10,378,194
1987	1,109,975	408,368	227,702	826,380	1,113,517	400,890	897,820	1,099,741	1,262,104	1,789,539	258,404	9,394,440
1988	2,011,039	612,156	599,942	1,063,640	1,633,469	617,421	611,945	769,670	1,459,951	2,351,336	424,529	12,155,098
1989	1,145,307	951,080	647,658	1,890,218	2,530,805	445,234	1,498,610	962,797	1,637,858	2,349,647	567,809	14,617,023
1990	1,311,546	587,544	661,077	2,453,121	1,443,906	752,692	1,200,643	1,008,733	2,202,626	2,433,593	655,291	14,710,772
1991	1,695,630	728,246	735,470	1,994,358	1,904,327	701,418	1,182,788	1,155,185	1,839,577	2,755,367	603,905	15,296,271
1992	2,034,595	851,819	507,614	2,428,210	2,072,963	474,766	1,255,371	1,822,054	1,866,495	2,863,504	578,829	16,756,220
1993	1,967,910	646,814	573,021	1,701,210	1,879,306	543,442	1,204,138	1,513,959	2,022,255	3,039,141	582,133	15,613,329
1994	2,252,935	740,444	587,173	1,947,656	2,151,807	622,251	1,378,813	1,733,392	2,315,508	3,479,424	666,811	17,876,214
Total	21,335,233	7,544,581	6,113,363	19,655,133	21,044,653	6,437,220	13,596,946	16,635,783	22,228,387	33,091,693	6,621,995	174,304,987

Total through 1989: $94.1 billion.

Table 3-20
Capital Requirements Assuming 7 Percent Inflation, 16-Year Aircraft Life, 5 Percent Growth
(thousands of dollars)

Year	American	Braniff	Continental	Delta	Eastern	National	Northwest	Pan American	Trans World	United	Western	Total
1977-1979	608,857	117,397	93,167	439,140	495,427	98,742	218,605	274,892	730,791	1,072,870	$ 321,280	4,471,168
1980	424,912	75,251	162,391	247,447	427,447	115,573	165,445	244,750	417,436	612,060	67,653	2,960,169
1981	499,771	84,322	67,012	275,261	425,153	172,972	291,391	442,856	420,169	697,676	126,418	3,503,001
1982	572,497	166,557	75,351	287,371	468,943	124,883	307,156	479,046	762,909	1,003,695	157,296	4,405,704
1983	920,346	428,803	84,529	484,955	636,748	150,742	262,265	814,215	758,362	1,209,236	172,812	5,923,013
1984	1,241,182	119,684	341,863	818,833	1,174,978	559,544	629,427	640,833	851,927	2,158,172	429,899	8,966,342
1985	1,175,081	209,885	147,831	791,237	709,071	113,108	580,493	760,812	973,619	1,667,219	400,174	7,528,530
1986	865,938	222,922	237,636	701,137	536,521	126,911	960,109	1,752,108	1,156,178	1,276,651	136,107	2,972,218
1987	753,169	291,073	134,614	517,595	772,259	302,291	679,367	825,199	895,458	1,238,094	152,917	6,562,036
1988	1,591,353	474,226	490,441	701,021	1,232,725	501,391	355,459	446,640	1,028,643	1,703,171	300,077	8,825,187
1989	652,304	788,849	509,225	1,463,911	2,060,110	309,140	1,196,680	583,356	1,131,111	1,588,288	422,026	10,705,000
1990	732,923	397,562	510,153	1,953,335	891,562	202,277	846,719	563,917	1,608,090	1,540,343	484,115	9,730,996
1991	1,017,946	505,361	558,761	1,408,253	1,256,567	514,390	767,974	633,572	1,142,803	1,708,529	403,464	9,917,620
1992	1,240,465	591,250	300,869	1,741,730	1,314,993	255,601	769,839	1,211,206	1,051,111	1,639,048	343,930	10,460,042
1993	1,039,628	341,423	270,835	898,452	992,668	286,784	635,886	799,805	1,067,982	1,604,926	313,365	8,251,754
1994	1,167,709	213,000	304,647	1,009,697	1,115,249	322,661	714,530	898,456	1,199,943	1,803,549	345,414	9,094,855
Total	14,504,081	5,027,565	4,289,325	13,739,375	14,510,215	4,157,010	9,381,355	11,371,663	15,196,572	22,523,527	4,576,947	119,277,635

Total through 1989: $71.8 billion.

Table 3-21
Capital Requirements Assuming 5 Percent Inflation, 18-Year Aircraft Life, 7 Percent Growth
(thousands of dollars)

Year	American	Braniff	Continental	Delta	Eastern	National	Northwest	Pan American	Trans World	United	Western	Total
1977–1979	729,796	160,320	127,204	491,380	592,173	134,735	298,459	375,318	667,897	1,224,993	170,741	4,973,015
1980	314,242	103,308	214,912	332,995	300,036	86,829	192,296	241,847	524,949	485,172	136,607	2,933,193
1981	352,984	115,991	92,005	305,132	362,769	97,494	215,991	271,600	362,889	579,595	134,964	2,891,415
1982	597,175	130,436	103,497	393,689	592,288	163,139	277,663	375,396	594,043	877,218	117,405	4,221,949
1983	689,264	146,431	116,171	438,503	605,984	225,369	407,191	588,880	614,535	991,335	182,348	5,006,011
1984	781,055	234,980	130,406	470,097	668,193	182,694	434,871	638,078	973,487	1,322,433	218,817	6,055,041
1985	1,200,571	496,068	146,645	683,761	853,178	214,527	425,139	978,210	988,654	1,552,750	240,781	7,780,284
1986	1,463,165	207,740	398,879	1,093,926	1,388,080	609,513	772,019	827,914	1,102,210	2,488,462	492,392	10,774,300
1987	1,422,302	303,363	223,244	1,020,750	974,054	196,218	741,535	961,101	1,243,834	2,059,411	469,516	9,615,328
1988	1,168,339	327,598	315,509	966,507	850,479	220,302	1,107,554	1,800,186	1,443,716	1,748,646	236,086	10,184,922
1989	1,107,743	403,216	233,608	838,345	1,105,627	390,346	873,782	1,072,482	1,247,379	1,178,242	265,167	8,715,937
1990	1,895,670	579,993	560,555	1,045,210	1,557,633	278,056	616,093	774,559	1,414,532	2,264,067	410,975	11,397,343
1991	1,131,097	867,518	587,416	1,754,280	2,320,314	423,554	1,380,292	940,799	1,560,094	2,248,005	532,018	13,745,387
1992	1,271,129	550,251	601,480	2,216,107	1,376,035	351,050	1,114,789	977,838	2,029,765	2,308,564	602,296	13,399,304
1993	1,589,493	664,342	658,128	1,813,012	1,754,293	632,625	1,093,165	1,098,522	1,713,789	2,445,922	548,833	14,012,124
1994	1,861,357	761,239	466,689	2,154,782	1,883,859	443,062	1,147,822	1,651,514	1,730,396	2,648,924	531,945	15,271,589
Total	17,575,382	6,052,794	4,976,348	15,948,476	17,184,995	4,649,443	11,098,661	13,564,244	18,212,169	26,423,740	5,290,890	140,977,142

Total through 989: $73.2 billion.

Table 3-22
Capital Requirements Assuming 5 Percent Inflation, 18-Year Aircraft Life, 5 Percent Growth
(thousands of dollars)

Year	American	Braniff	Continental	Delta	Eastern	National	Northwest	Pan American	Trans World	United	Western	Total
1977-1979	585,880	112,967	89,651	366,858	454,653	95,016	210,355	264,518	519,957	1,002,670	128,132	3,830,657
1980	212,185	69,781	150,586	244,802	202,524	58,530	121,719	163,201	420,050	327,539	106,376	2,077,293
1981	233,771	76,730	60,979	234,368	248,807	64,559	143,079	179,833	240,335	395,466	99,762	1,977,689
1982	458,344	84,827	67,286	273,528	459,847	124,923	192,710	268,641	451,327	662,706	76,307	3,120,446
1983	527,835	93,410	74,071	299,045	451,791	180,769	308,518	464,816	448,633	742,153	134,590	3,725,631
1984	593,872	173,368	81,642	300,195	489,299	130,959	320,213	423,996	781,055	1,033,164	163,422	4,561,185
1985	983,577	424,849	90,075	496,213	645,903	154,622	292,274	811,114	765,714	1,217,686	176,525	6,058,552
1986	1,211,867	125,192	333,389	806,896	1,148,509	540,063	618,346	634,795	844,058	2,100,854	418,069	8,782,038
1987	1,132,372	208,052	147,603	769,840	696,758	16,100	564,027	738,017	945,909	1,611,324	383,801	7,313,803
1988	833,688	217,615	228,194	677,361	530,941	127,782	903,036	1,554,873	1,099,830	1,231,810	136,849	7,541,979
1989	721,981	276,275	133,113	504,770	737,320	283,856	637,530	775,579	850,862	1,182,498	151,096	6,254,880
1990	1,451,372	434,116	444,668	661,448	1,133,514	455,220	344,331	433,005	958,017	1,578,182	279,537	8,173,410
1991	620,461	699,574	454,266	1,312,648	1,832,226	282,629	1,067,729	547,763	1,035,074	1,459,211	380,985	9,692,566
1992	683,936	357,581	448,610	1,708,513	815,580	188,996	755,779	526,167	1,428,856	1,402,160	428,608	8,742,786
1993	915,935	442,752	482,398	1,230,534	1,110,952	446,395	680,844	580,335	1,021,373	1,454,818	355,959	8,722,295
1994	1,088,642	507,193	265,522	1,486,926	1,145,797	229,744	674,832	1,047,013	936,079	1,455,648	298,600	9,135,996
Total	12,255,718	4,304,282	3,552,053	11,373,945	12,104,421	3,480,163	7,835,322	9,483,666	12,745,129	18,857,889	3,718,618	99,711,206

Total through 1989: $55.2 billion.

Table 3-23

Capital Requirements Assuming 5 Percent Inflation, 16-Year Aircraft Life, 7 Percent Growth

(thousands of dollars)

Year	American	Braniff	Continental	Delta	Eastern	National	Northwest	Pan American	Trans World	United	Western	Total
1977-												
1979	729,796	160,320	127,204	547,089	614,250	134,735	298,459	375,318	851,326	1,254,705	236,766	5,329,968
1980	496,082	103,308	214,912	317,652	493,696	135,471	224,004	305,605	491,991	725,201	92,966	3,600,888
1981	573,987	115,991	92,005	354,297	500,836	190,335	338,068	494,750	504,894	820,169	150,239	4,135,571
1982	651,054	194,339	103,497	376,774	551,190	149,732	359,232	534,526	823,966	1,110,776	181,558	5,036,644
1983	1,024,357	428,767	116,171	564,410	712,156	176,690	346,013	837,536	830,432	1,308,799	199,188	6,544,519
1984	1,254,468	164,527	342,730	866,012	1,189,817	532,814	655,898	695,131	924,999	2,145,069	425,063	9,196,528
1985	1,208,548	248,324	181,311	855,209	805,602	155,347	622,695	809,083	1,044,498	1,741,893	401,931	8,074,441
1986	968,336	267,138	262,264	707,606	683,836	174,538	948,689	1,643,948	1,215,522	1,444,737	187,027	8,593,641
1987	901,932	331,828	185,024	671,491	904,810	325,751	729,541	893,616	1,025,548	1,454,125	209,971	7,633,637
1988	1,603,569	488,123	478,384	848,129	1,302,501	492,321	487,955	584,497	1,164,141	1,874,917	338,513	9,663,050
1989	896,174	744,196	498,952	1,479,048	1,980,291	348,385	1,172,625	753,364	1,281,583	1,838,540	44,296	11,037,454
1990	1,007,175	451,147	507,610	1,883,637	1,108,708	577,957	921,918	774,559	1,691,293	1,868,642	503,167	11,295,813
1991	1,277,660	548,735	554,177	1,502,752	1,434,913	528,519	891,232	870,434	1,386,124	2,076,173	455,044	11,525,763
1992	1,504,414	629,850	375,338	1,795,459	1,532,783	351,050	928,242	1,347,257	1,380,117	2,118,344	427,996	12,390,850
1993	1,427,908	469,326	372,246	1,234,391	1,363,616	394,309	873,717	1,098,522	1,467,339	2,100,179	422,393	11,223,956
1994	1,604,160	527,220	418,085	1,386,792	1,532,154	443,062	981,758	1,234,229	1,648,714	2,477,459	474,790	12,728,423
Total	17,129,620	5,873,139	4,829,910	15,480,748	16,711,159	5,111,026	10,780,046	13,252,375	17,732,487	26,359,728	4,750,908	138,011,146

Total through 1989: $78.8 billion.

Table 3-24
Capital Requirements Assuming 5 Percent Inflation, 16-Year Aircraft Life, 5 Percent Growth
(thousands of dollars)

Year	American	Braniff	Continental	Delta	Eastern	National	Northwest	Pan American	Trans World	United	Western	Total
1977-1979	585,880	112,967	89,651	422,568	476,730	95,016	210,355	264,518	703,386	1,032,382	194,158	4,187,611
1980	394,025	69,781	150,586	229,459	396,183	107,172	153,428	226,959	387,092	567,568	62,735	2,744,988
1981	454,774	76,730	60,979	250,478	386,874	157,399	265,156	402,984	382,340	633,653	115,036	3,186,403
1982	511,220	148,730	67,286	256,612	418,749	111,516	274,280	427,771	681,251	896,264	140,640	3,934,139
1983	862,928	375,747	74,071	424,952	557,963	132,090	247,340	713,472	664,530	1,056,616	151,340	5,264,049
1984	1,067,285	102,916	293,966	704,110	1,010,923	481,149	541,240	551,048	732,567	1,855,800	369,668	7,710,672
1985	991,555	177,105	124,742	667,661	598,327	95,442	489,830	641,987	821,558	1,406,830	337,674	6,352,711
1986	717,038	184,590	196,774	580,575	444,265	105,088	795,016	1,450,829	957,370	1,057,128	112,703	6,601,376
1987	612,002	236,517	109,383	420,582	627,514	245,633	552,003	670,532	727,622	1,006,038	124,256	5,332,112
1988	1,268,919	378,140	391,069	558,982	982,963	399,801	283,437	339,184	820,255	1,358,080	239,276	7,020,106
1989	510,412	617,254	398,456	1,145,473	1,611,984	241,895	936,372	456,461	885,066	1,242,795	330,225	8,376,393
1990	562,777	305,269	391,722	1,499,875	684,589	155,319	650,155	433,005	1,234,777	1,182,757	371,729	7,471,974
1991	767,023	380,790	421,027	1,061,120	946,825	387,594	578,669	477,397	861,103	1,287,379	304,010	7,472,937
1992	917,221	437,180	222,468	1,287,865	972,328	188,996	569,232	895,586	777,209	1,211,940	254,307	7,734,332
1993	754,350	247,735	196,517	651,913	720,276	208,089	461,397	580,335	774,923	1,109,074	227,377	5,931,986
1994	831,445	151,663	216,918	718,936	794,092	229,744	508,768	639,729	854,397	1,284,183	245,946	6,475,821
Total	11,808,854	4,003,114	3,405,615	10,881,161	11,630,585	3,341,943	7,516,708	9,171,797	12,265,446	18,191,487	3,580,900	95,797,610

Total through 1989: $60.7 billion.

Table 3-25
Projected Cost to Replace One Seat
(dollars)

	Cost Per Seat		
Year	5 Percent Inflation	8 Percent Inflation	7 Percent Inflation
1977-1979	103,166	109,274	107,212
1980	113,650	127,206	122,559
1981	119,332	137,382	131,389
1982	125,299	148,373	140,318
1983	131,564	160,243	150,141
1984	138,142	173,062	160,650
1985	145,049	186,907	171,896
1986	152,302	201,860	183,929
1987	159,917	218,008	196,804
1988	167,913	235,449	210,580
1989	176,308	254,285	225,321
1990	185,124	274,628	241,093
1991	194,380	296,598	257,969
1992	204,099	320,326	276,027
1993	214,304	345,952	295,349
1994	225,019	373,628	316,024

One statement in Pan American's 1976 Form 10-K foreshadows what some believe to be the dubious status of the industry's financial credibility. "Pan Am's Loan and Credit Agreements generally prohibit Pan Am from acquiring, leasing, or creating security interests in additional aircraft."[25]

The lenders, however, agreed to waive this restriction with respect to three aircraft previously ordered.

It is estimated that 91 percent of Pan American's December 31, 1976 fleet will require replacement prior to 1990. Sixty-five percent will come due for replacement in the 1985-1988 period, assuming as indicated an eighteen-year aircraft life. While earlier phase-out of the 707-300 aircraft than has been indicated might be desirable, the estimate appears accurate in light of Pan American's overall condition. It is against this ominous background that capital needs of $4.76 billion for replacement and $4.88 billion for growth capital requirements are projected for the period ending in 1989.

Like Pan American and Eastern, Trans World Airlines is a financially troubled airline. In its 1976 Form 10-K, the company indicated that it was unable to comply with various debt tests in its loan agreements "and thus was prohibited from borrowing additional amounts under the July 1973 Loan Agreement."[26]

Management, in discussing the problem of capital formation, indicates the following with respect to TWA's relative competitive position. "It would also be necessary for other airlines to raise substantial funds for future aircraft needs, but some of TWA's competitors are in a substantially better position to raise

Table 3-26
Increased Cost per Seat For Selected Carriers
Due to Inflation
(thousands of dollars)

Year	American	Eastern	Pan American	Trans World	United	Average
1968	36.0	36.5	33.6	37.8	37.6	36.3
1969	42.6	–	38.7	39.1	40.3	40.2
1970	–	46.2	54.8	–	57.5	52.8
1971	62.0	–	61.8	–	59.9	61.2
1972	64.7	57.0	–	65.6	60.4	61.9
1973	–	59.0	–	68.9	63.2	63.7
1974	–	–	–	71.2	69.0	70.1
1975	68.0	65.0	–	73.8	74.8	70.4
1976	72.0	–	77.9	–	–	75.0

Note: These are the costs of aircraft delivered in these years. The cost of placing an order for future aircraft delivery is higher. In addition, these prices do not include the cost of spare parts and support equipment, which are typically 20 percent additional to the basic price of the aircraft (see ATA study).

Annual Rate of Inflation = 9.5 percent.

funds for capital expenditures than TWA."[27] On December 31, 1976 TWA had contracted to purchase eleven L-1011's and thirty-one B-727's, or 6,467 aircraft seats. The estimates developed herein place TWA's 1977-1979 requirements at 5,757 seats, with an additional 1,778 seats needed in 1980 just for replacing obsolete capacity. This purchase is therefore required for the immediate future. TWA's financial condition seriously threatened the acquisition. "An aircraft delivery deferral agreement with delivery dates unspecified was signed March 31, 1976 by TWA and Boeing Aircraft Company."[28]

The penalty to TWA for having to defer those aircraft from their scheduled 1976-1977 delivery was $4,614,000. Management indicates that "these aircraft will be needed in future years to handle traffic growth and to replace aircraft as circumstances require, assuming that suitable financing can be arranged for their acquisition."[29]

This study estimates that Trans World, for the period ending in 1989, will require $4.56 billion for aircraft replacement and $6.51 billion for additional capacity to meet growing demand.

United, the nation's largest carrier, faces large replacement needs in the years ahead. This study projects that $9.4 billion will be required for aircraft replacement and $12.0 billion for increased capacity prior to 1990.

With respect to noise regulation, United indicates that:

Compliance with this regulation . . . could require expensive modification or premature retirement or replacement of all the aircraft in United's fleet except six of the eighteen Boeing 747's and all of the DC-10's, which meet the prescribed noise limits.[30]

Table 3-27
Demand for Air Travel: 1966-1975
(Revenue Passenger Miles, thousands of dollars)

Year	Domestic Operations	Foreign Operations	Total
1966	56,802,788	19,298,420	76,101,208
1967	70,990,141	23,259,314	94,249,455
1968	81,611,832	26,450,644	108,062,476
1969	95,657,705	22,702,695	118,360,400
1970	95,899,744	27,563,211	123,462,955
1971	97,756,113	29,219,294	126,975,407
1972	108,189,968	34,268,298	142,458,266
1973	115,352,180	35,369,973	150,992,153
1974	117,616,261	33,186,199	150,802,460
1975	119,445,956	31,081,668	150,527,624
1976	131,424,511	33,716,743	165,141,254

Source: 1966-1975 data from *Air Transport 1976* (Washington: Air Transport Association Press, pp. 13 and 16). 1976 data from *Aviation Daily*, March 11, 1977, p. 73.

Percentage increase in total revenue passenger miles from 76,101,208 in 1966 to 150,552,624 in 1975 is 7.1 percent per year.

One of the principal culprits is the JT3D engine, which powers various aircraft, including United's DC-8-61's and DC-8-62's. The present study assumes that sixteen DC-8-61's and four DC-8-62's will be used into 1986-1987. It is possible, however, that these aircraft will have to be phased out earlier.

On June 30, 1977 United had contracted to purchase forty-six B-727's to "replace less efficient DC-8 nonfan aircraft and 23 Boeing 727-100 aircraft."[31] This should provide approximately 5,796 seats. This covers the present study's estimate of capacity replacement prior to 1980, and will provide about 16 percent of the additional capacity required for growth. Additional purchases are also discussed in the next chapter.

Western is a successful though leveraged carrier, which will experience capital needs of $1.12 billion for aircraft replacement and $1.88 billion for capacity expansion prior to 1990. On March 15, 1977 Western had ordered ten B-727-200 aircraft and two DC-10 aircraft for a total of 1,728 seats. This coincides with estimates developed here that the company will require approximately 1,450 seats prior to 1980. Western also disclosed options for the purchase of an identical aircraft combination. According to this study, the exercise of those options would satisfy capacity requirements into 1981-1982.

The largest number of aircraft come due for replacement in 1986, in which year it is estimated that Western will incur capital requirements for replacement and expansion of $404.5 million and $198.6 million, respectively.

Table 3-12 summarizes the capital requirements discussed in this chapter. Replacement needs for the period December 31, 1976 to December 31, 1989 will be $33.4 billion, and capital required for growth will be $48.1 billion. The total bill for the domestic trunk carriers and Pan American is estimated to be $81.5 billion.

Notes

1. Civil Aeronautics Board, *Airline Equipment Needs and Financing Through 1985* (CAB, Washington, Bureau of Accounts & Statistics, 1976).

2. Donaldson, Lufkin, and Jenrette, *Domestic Trunk Airlines: A Shortage Industry in the Making* (New York: Donaldson, Lufkin and Jenrette, 1976).

3. Air Transport Association, *The Sixty Billion Dollar Question* (Washington: ATA, Economics and Finance Dept., 1976), p. 3.

4. ATA, *The Sixty Billion Dollar Question*, p. 3. Reprinted by permission.

5. All amounts, dates, and related aircraft data are available in the *Form 41*'s for December 31, 1976 filed by the respective carriers.

6. A longer lead time was assumed for the 747 and DC-10 because this was the period immediately subsequent to their development.

7. Taken from Boeing's price listing issued to assist the various airlines with their replacement cost information requirements for the SEC.

8. ATA, *The Sixty Billion Dollar Question*, p. 3. Reprinted with permission.

9. 1966-75 data from *Air Transport 1976* (Washington, D.C.: Air Transport Association, 1976), pp. 13 and 16. 1976 data from *Aviation Daily*, March 11, 1977 (Washington, D.C.: Ziff-Davis Publishers, 1977), p. 73.

10. ATA, *The Sixty Billion Dollar Question*, p. 3. Reprinted with permission.

11. NASA, *Outlook for Aeronautics* (Virginia: National Technical Information Services, 1976).

12. *Aviation Daily*, December 1976.

13. *Aviation Daily*, January 18, 1977.

14. *Form 10-K*, 1976, American Airlines, p. 22.

15. Ibid., p. 27.

16. Continental Airlines, 1976 *Annual Report*, p. 1.

17. Delta has a June 30 year end for fiscal purposes.

18. Delta, *Form 10-K*.

19. *Wall Street Journal*, March 9, 1978, p. 1.

20. Ibid., p. 1.

21. Donaldson, Lufkin, and Jenrette, *Domestic Trunk Airlines: A Shortage Industry in the Making*, p. 41.

22. National Airlines, 1976 *Form 10-K*, p. 13.

23. Ibid., p. 9.

24. Northwest Airlines, 1976 *Form 10-K*, p. 9.

25. Pan American World Airways, 1976 *Form 10-K*, p. 1.

26. Trans World Airlines, 1976 *Form 10-K*, p. 9.

27. Ibid., p. 9.

28. Ibid., p. 9.

29. Trans World Airlines, 1976 *Form 10-K*, Note 7.

30. United Airlines, September 30, 1977 *Prospectus*, "Airline Operation" section.

31. United, *Prospectus*, Note 12.

4 Forecasted Capital Availability

In the previous chapter, the industry's probable capital needs were determined. The task now is to quantify capital available for investment in new aircraft, by carrier, over the same period. The following discussion details the methodology employed, and then turns to a carrier-by-carrier analysis of the findings.

The question is whether, given the data as of December 31, 1976, and given alternative historical trends, the industry will be able to finance its capital needs for expansion and replacement. The approach taken in this chapter can be outlined as follows:

1. Estimate operating earnings and, one step removed, internally generated funds available for capital investment.
2. Develop shareholders' equity estimates by year consistent with the operating earnings less fixed interest charges and debt retirement.
3. Develop estimates of possible new debt based on a more realistic debt-to-equity relationship than now exists (a 55/45 ratio is assumed). Actual December 31, 1976 ratios appear in table 4-1.
4. Contrast, on a first simulation basis, projected funds available with the capital needs developed in chapter 3. Assume that the new debt deemed possible in step three is floated as required to meet capital needs.
5. Calculate, as a second simulation, the status of capital requirements after this new debt is floated, taking into account interest expense on cumulative new debt (a 10 percent annual rate is assumed).

Two options were selected for operating earnings, measured by the operating ratio (operating expenses divided by operating revenues). One was the ratio that prevailed in 1976. The other was the ratio that characterized the five-year period ending December 31, 1976. For certain carriers, the five-year period was the more favorable one. For most, however, the year 1976 showed performance above the five-year average. Best case and worst case simulations appear for the airlines in question using these earnings trends as a basis.

The same growth in constant dollar operating earnings was assumed as was used for capacity growth requirements—6 percent. A price inflation of 7 percent annually was assumed for both expenses and revenues. This is somewhat less than the 8 percent inflation that was assumed for price increases in aircraft to be acquired, a conservative differential in light of recent history and the sophisticated changes forthcoming to achieve operating economies and comply with environmental standards. Tables 4-2 to 4-23 depict the projected operating

Table 4-1
Capital Structure by Airline on December 31, 1976
(thousands of dollars)

Company	Equity	Long-Term Debt	Financing Leases	Debt Plus Leases	Debt/Equity Ratio
American	610,074	416,255	778,000	1,194,255	66/34
Braniff	184,434	235,265	178,008	413,273	69/31
Continental	156,639	327,823	–	327,823	68/32
Delta	542,112	350,968	194,920	545,888	50/50
Eastern	298,614	566,042	761,100	1,327,142	82/18
National	193,931	141,425	118,763	260,188	57/43
Northwest	665,744	122,000	–	122,000	16/84
Pan American	352,152	727,305	588,700	1,316,005	79/21
Trans World	377,100	907,500	656,408	1,563,908	81/19
United	799,000	932,225	819,766	1,751,991	69/31
Western	117,100	110,420	118,798	229,218	66/34

earnings by year for each carrier. To this must be added noncash expense, namely, depreciation. Depreciation charges to income were calculated for the December 31, 1976 fleet and all additions thereto, as determined by the estimates in this study. Residual values were added in the year in which the aircraft will terminate, in an amount estimated by the respective companies.

From the subtotal of operating earnings and the estimates just described, debt retirements and interest on outstanding debt levels were subtracted, thereby arriving at total internally generated funds available for capital investment.

Estimates of shareholders' equity by year are arrived at by taking the December 31, 1976 balances, adding operating earnings, and subtracting interest expense and debt amortization. Because of the need to be competitive with many conservatively financed and profitable industrial concerns, it is assumed that a reasonable level of debt to equity must be maintained. Rationalization of capital structure is a necessary cost for several of the carriers. It is therefore assumed that the debt-to-equity ratio for each carrier will reach equilibrium at 55/45. For Delta and Northwest, this is higher than their present relative debt levels, and will in their cases add to available capital. For the others, reducing risk in financial structure will further reduce the capital available for investment until a one-time debt retirement equal to the excessive leverage has been achieved.

The next step develops estimates of possible new debt. Inputs to this calculation are (1) the equity estimates developed here; (2) the amount of old debt outstanding; (3) the present value of financing leases by year; and (4) the capital structure parameter (debt to equity ratio of 55/45).

Table 4-2
Projected Operating Earnings for American Airlines Assuming Worst Case
(thousands of dollars)

Year	Internally Generated Funds	Total Capital Requirements	New Debt Required (Retired)	New Debt Possible	Surplus	Cumulative Surplus
1977-						
1979	65,663	696,785.5	631,122.5	—	(631,122.5)	(631,122.5)
1980	52,527	294,609.5	242,082.5	—	(242,082.5)	(873,205.0)
1981	68,200	337,753.5	269,553.5	—	(269,553.5)	(1,142,758.5)
1982	62,978	624,947.0	561,969.0	91,762	(470,207.0)	(1,612,965.5)
1983	81,102	741,204.0	660,102.0	125,632	(534,470.0)	(2,147,435.5)
1984	100,822	861,243.5	760,421.5	135,831	(624,590.5)	(2,772,026.0)
1985	136,665	1,407,222.5	1,270,557.5	148,034	(1,122,523.5)	(3,894,549.5)
1986	173,123	1,772,734.5	1,599,611.5	161,448	(1,438,163.5)	(5,332,713.0)
1987	201,763	1,741,339.0	1,539,576.0	98,176	(1,441,400.0)	(6,774,113.0)
1988	224,072	1,403,629.0	1,179,557.0	200,325	(979,232.0)	(7,753,345.0)
1989	265,391	1,319,485.0	1,054,094.0	48,414	(1,005,680.0)	(8,759,025.0)
1990	312,326	2,487,137.5	2,174,811.5	154,534	(2,020,277.5)	(10,779,302.5)
1991	392,349	1,336,322.5	943,973.5	178,246	(765,727.5)	(11,545,030.0)
1992	479,122	1,534,201.0	1,055,079.0	205,802	(849,277.0)	(12,394,307.0)
1993	559,052	2,022,262.5	1,463,210.5	90,211	(1,372,999.5)	(13,767,307.0)
1994	649,265	2,449,131.5	1,799,866.5	327,784	(1,472,082.5)	(15,239,389.5)

Note: Parentheses indicate shortfalls.

Table 4-3
Projected Operating Earnings for Braniff International Corporation Assuming Worst Case
(thousands of dollars)

Year	Internally Generated Funds	Total Capital Requirements	New Debt Required (Retired)	New Debt Possible	Surplus	Cumulative Surplus
1977-						
1979	201,150	144,733.5	(56,416.5)	4,899	61,315.5	61,315.5
1980	105,750	96,867.0	(8,883.0)	132,926	141,809.0	263,124.5
1981	134,470	110,936.0	(23,534.0)	123,768	147,302.0	350,426.5
1982	137,807	127,452.0	(10,355.0)	142,192	152,547.0	502,973.5
1983	165,713	146,061.5	(19,651.5)	163,207	182,858.5	685,832.0
1984	198,115	255,785.5	57,670.0	186,092	128,422.0	814,254.0
1985	248,115	593,336.5	345,221.5	211,818	(133,403.5)	680,850.5
1986	297,261	220,633.0	(76,628.0)	240,239	316,867.0	997,717.5
1987	347,735	348,594.5	859.5	254,453	253,593.5	1,251,311.0
1988	385,378	382,251.5	(3,126.5)	289,788	292,914.5	1,544,225.5
1989	468,068	490,007.5	21,939.5	359,235	337,295.5	1,881,521.0
1990	510,604	752,206.5	241,602.5	375,041	133,438.5	2,014,959.5
1991	613,206	1,195,586.5	582,380.0	426,049	(156,331.0)	1,858,628.5
1992	719,809	712,405.0	(7,404.0)	483,466	490,870.0	2,349,498.5
1993	824,210	893,594.0	69,384.0	549,728	480,344.0	2,829,842.5
1994	945,856	1,053,071.0	107,215.0	624,054	516,839.0	3,346,681.5

Note: Parentheses indicate shortfalls.

Table 4-4
Projected Operating Earnings for Continental Airlines Assuming Worst Case
(thousands of dollars)

Year	Internally Generated Funds	Total Capital Requirements	New Debt Required (Retired)	New Debt Possible	Surplus	Cumulative Surplus
1977-1979	33,832	114,847.0	81,015.0	—	(81,015.0)	(81,015.0)
1980	74,977	204,547.5	129,570.5	—	(129,570.5)	(210,585.5)
1981	101,844	88,062.0	(13,782.0)	—	13,782.0	(196,803.5)
1982	112,509	101,116.0	(11,393.0)	25,801	37,194.0	(159,609.5)
1983	131,654	125,230.0	(6,424.0)	81,158	87,582.0	(72,027.5)
1984	153,840	132,825.5	(21,014.5)	96,956	117,970.5	45,943.0
1985	189,601	152,516.0	(37,085.0)	112,135	149,220.0	195,163.0
1986	227,031	485,271.5	258,240.5	129,457	(128,783.5)	66,379.5
1987	233,598	252,780.0	19,182.0	147,579	128,397.0	194,776.5
1988	266,065	381,273.0	115,208.0	169,106	53,898.0	248,674.5
1989	292,524	264,456.0	(28,068.0)	192,769	220,837.0	469,511.5
1990	343,596	745,615.0	402,019.0	219,479	(182,540.0)	286,971.5
1991	416,355	794,734.5	378,379.5	249,576	(128,803.5)	158,168.0
1992	497,429	824,039.0	326,610.0	284,043	(42,567.0)	115,601.0
1993	584,714	920,578.5	335,864.5	322,959	(12,905.5)	102,695.5
1994	667,972	607,892.5	(60,079.5)	366,339	426,418.5	529,114.0

Note: Parentheses indicate shortfall.

Table 4-5
Projected Operating Earnings for Delta Airlines Assuming Worst Case
(thousands of dollars)

Year	Internally Generated Funds	Total Capital Requirements	New Debt Required (Retired)	New Debt Possible	Surplus	Cumulative Surplus
1977-						
1979	664,607	454,525.0	(210,082)	623,568	833,650.0	833,650.0
1980	297,765	323,358.0	25,593.0	270,909	245,316.0	1,078,966.0
1981	395,200	292,005.5	(103,194.5)	287,415	390,609.5	1,469,575.0
1982	436,413	395,043.0	(41,370.0)	324,711	366,081.0	1,835,656.5
1983	489,259	449,161.0	(40,098.0)	367,560	407,658.0	2,243,314.5
1984	525,934	487,515.5	(38,418.5)	414,424	452,842.5	2,696,157.0
1985	564,018	760,244.5	196,226.5	469,083	272,856.5	2,969,013.5
1986	630,341	1,213,279.5	582,938.5	528,051	(54,887.5)	2,914,126.0
1987	690,902	1,220,518.0	529,616	576,592	46,076.0	2,961,102.0
1988	799,863	1,152,522.5	352,659.5	655,151	302,491.5	3,263,593.5
1989	924,003	968,571.5	44,568.5	744,198	699,129.5	3,963,223.0
1990	1,065,245	1,265,898.0	200,563.0	844,891	644,238.0	4,607,461.0
1991	1,225,764	2,339,861.5	1,104,097.5	958,520	(115,577.5)	4,451,883.5
1992	1,405,013	3,079,774.5	1,674,761.5	1,086,487	(588,274.5)	3,863,609.0
1993	1,617,931	2,456,605.0	838,674.0	1,234,243	395,569.0	4,259,178.0
1994	1,856,170	3,023,398.0	1,167,228.0	1,400,042	232,814.0	4,491,992.0

Note: Parentheses indicate shortfalls.

Table 4-6
Projected Operating Earnings for Eastern Airlines Assuming Worst Case
(thousands of dollars)

Year	Internally Generated Funds	Total Capital Requirements	New Debt Required (Retired)	New Debt Possible	Surplus	Cumulative Surplus
1977						
1979	82,561	554,402.0	471,841.0	—	(471,841.0)	(471,841.0)
1980	92,489	281,252.5	183,763.5	—	(183,763.5)	(655,604.5)
1981	172,515	352,041.0	179,526.0	—	(179,526.0)	(835,130.5)
1982	211,564	622,944.0	411,380.0	—	(411,380.0)	(1,246,510.5)
1983	258,458	644,176.5	385,718.5	24,126	(361,592.5)	(1,608,103.0)
1984	320,975	725,043.5	404,068.0	208,306	(195,762.0)	(1,803,065.0)
1985	390,874	965,842.0	574,968.0	258,818	(316,150.0)	(2,119,215.0)
1986	490,483	1,680,989.0	1,190,506.0	69,251	(1,121,255.0)	(3,240,470.0)
1987	595,239	1,138,874.0	543,635.0	214,765	(328,870.0)	(3,569,340.0)
1988	667,136	968,519.5	301,383.0	246,291	(55,092.0)	(3,624,432.0)
1989	765,488	1,329,020.5	563,532.5	281,508	(282,024.5)	(3,906,456.5)
1990	897,021	1,996,133.5	1,099,112.5	321,940	(777,172.5)	(4,683,629.0)
1991	1,090,523	3,168,111.5	2,077,858.5	367,093	(1,710,765.5)	(6,394,394.5)
1992	1,291,967	1,719,330.5	427,363.5	421,933	(5,430.5)	(6,399,825.0)
1993	1,463,296	2,101,122.5	637,826.5	474,794	(163,032.5)	(6,562,857.5)
1994	1,601,901	1,514,828.0	87,073.0	542,720	629,793.0	(5,933,064.5)

Note: Parentheses indicate shortfalls.

Table 4-7
Projected Operating Earnings for National Airlines Assuming Worst Case
(thousands of dollars)

Year	Internally Generated Funds	Total Capital Requirements	New Debt Required (Retired)	New Debt Possible	Surplus	Cumulative Surplus
1977-1979	105,713	121,676.5	15,963.5	75,932	59,968.5	59,968.5
1980	46,565	81,348.0	34,783.0	21,088	(13,695.0)	46,273.5
1981	54,709	93,282.5	38,573.5	8,723	(29,850.5)	16,423.0
1982	66,068	170,355.0	104,287.0	14,246	(90,041.0)	(73,618.0)
1983	81,970	247,335.0	165,365.0	38,677	(126,688.0)	(200,306.0)
1984	98,453	196,425.5	97,972.5	42,241	(55,731.5)	(256,037.5)
1985	114,963	237,839.0	122,876.0	46,321	(76,555.0)	(332,592.5)
1986	146,764	761,820.0	615,056.0	50,992	(564,064.0)	(896,656.5)
1987	171,891	212,885.0	40,994.0	44,216	3,222.0	(893,434.5)
1988	187,680	244,043.0	56,363.0	50,240	(6,123.0)	(899,557.5)
1989	216,498	486,193.0	269,695.0	57,066	(212,629.0)	(1,112,186.5)
1990	255,297	766,349.5	511,052.5	64,792	(446,260.5)	(1,558,447.0)
1991	303,211	538,770.0	235,559.0	73,504	(162,055.0)	(1,720,502.0)
1992	341,320	423,791.5	82,471.5	83,318	846.5	(1,719,655.5)
1993	391,050	870,934.0	479,884.0	94,647	(385,237.0)	(2,104,892.5)
1994	446,122	558,574.0	112,452.0	107,359	(5,093.0)	(2,109,985.5)

Note: Parentheses indicate shortfalls.

Table 4-8
Projected Operating Earnings for Northwest Airlines Assuming Worst Case
(thousands of dollars)

Year	Internally Generated Funds	Total Capital Requirements	New Debt Required (Retired)	New Debt Possible	Surplus	Cumulative Surplus
1977–1979	545,421	269,470.0	(275,951.0)	953,570	1,229,521.0	1,229,521.0
1980	241,449	175,735.5	(65,713.5)	177,576	243,289.5	1,472,810.5
1981	267,443	206,691.0	(60,752.0)	190,101	250,853.0	1,723,663.5
1982	307,459	278,496.5	(28,962.5)	216,752	245,714.5	1,969,378.0
1983	356,572	435,861.0	79,289.0	271,198	191,909.0	2,161,287.0
1984	406,638	472,978.5	66,340.5	263,532	197,191.5	2,358,478.5
1985	441,748	462,221.0	20,473.0	320,588	300,115.0	2,658,593.5
1986	504,608	921,390.0	416,782.0	362,921	(53,861.0)	2,604,732.5
1987	603,778	889,908.5	286,130.5	401,231	115,100.5	2,719,833.0
1988	696,616	1,409,633.5	713,017.5	455,901	(257,116.5)	2,462,716.5
1989	814,975	1,089,865.5	274,890.5	517,865	242,974.5	2,705,691.0
1990	922,467	712,385.0	(210,082.0)	587,932	798,014.0	3,503,705.0
1991	1,061,876	1,867,677.5	805,801.5	667,006	(138,795.5)	3,364,909.5
1992	1,238,979	1,467,894.0	228,915.0	756,052	527,137.0	3,892,046.5
1993	1,413,721	1,431,895.5	18,174.5	858,869	840,694.5	4,732,741.0
1994	1,600,153	1,513,193.0	(86,960.0)	974,245	1,061,245.0	5,793,946.0

Note: Parentheses indicate shortfalls.

Table 4-9
Projected Operating Earnings for Pan American World Airways Assuming Worst Case
(thousands of dollars)

Year	Internally Generated Funds	Total Capital Requirements	New Debt Required (Retired)	New Debt Possible	Surplus	Cumulative Surplus
1977-						
1979	—	338,859.0	338,859.0	—	(338,859.0)	(338,859.0)
1980	—	226,681.0	226,681.0	—	(226,681.0)	(565,540.0)
1981	—	259,858.0	259,858.0	—	(259,858.0)	(825,398.0)
1982	—	381,319.0	381,319.0	—	(381,319.0)	(1,206,717.0)
1983	—	641,693.5	641,693.5	—	(641,693.5)	(1,848,410.5)
1984	—	709,121.5	709,121.5	—	(709,121.5)	(2,557,532.0)
1985	—	1,152,842.5	1,152,842.5	—	(1,152,842.5)	(3,710,374.5)
1986	—	970,341.0	970,341.0	—	(970,341.0)	(4,680,715.5)
1987	—	1,158,167.5	1,158,167.5	—	(1,158,167.5)	(5,838,883.0)
1988	—	2,469,860.0	2,469,860.0	—	(2,469,860.0)	(8,308,743.0)
1989	—	1,332,708.0	1,332,708.0	—	(1,332,708.0)	(9,641,451.0)
1990	—	895,699.5	895,699.5	—	(895,699.5)	(10,537,150.5)
1991	—	1,144,673.5	1,144,673.5	—	(1,144,673.5)	(11,681,824.0)
1992	—	1,180,241.0	1,180,241.0	—	(1,180,241.0)	(12,862,065.0)
1993	—	1,355,094.0	1,355,094.0	—	(1,355,094.0)	(14,217,159.0)
1994	—	2,232,053.5	2,232,053.5	—	(2,232,053.5)	(16,449,212.5)

Note: Parentheses indicate shortfalls.

Table 4-10
Projected Operating Earnings for Trans World Airlines Assuming Worst Case
(thousands of dollars)

Year	Internally Generated Funds	Total Capital Requirements	New Debt Required (Retired)	New Debt Possible	Surplus	Cumulative Surplus
1977-						
1979	—	629,090.5	629,090.5	—	(629,090.5)	(629,090.5)
1980	89,770	528,859.0	439,089.0	—	(439,089.0)	(1,068,179.5)
1981	145,273	347,233.0	201,960.0	—	(201,960.0)	(1,270,139.5)
1982	206,456	618,938.0	412,482.0	—	(412,482.0)	(1,862,621.5)
1983	245,073	647,462.0	402,389.0	—	(402,389.0)	(2,085,010.5)
1984	319,199	1,099,030.5	779,831.5	—	(779,831.5)	(2,864,842.0)
1985	394,745	1,130,320.0	735,575.0	—	(735,575.0)	(3,600,417.0)
1986	491,607	1,289,784.5	798,177.5	—	(798,177.5)	(4,398,594.5)
1987	547,773	1,492,591.5	944,818.5	—	(944,818.5)	(5,343,413.0)
1988	670,585	1,783,291.0	1,112,706.0	33,121	(1,079,585.0)	(6,422,998.0)
1989	777,018	1,513,122.5	736,104.5	160,156	(575,948.5)	(6,998,946.5)
1990	893,410	1,759,816.5	866,406.0	185,690	(680,716.0)	(7,679,662.5)
1991	1,025,018	1,979,940.0	954,922.0	213,404	(742,518.0)	(8,422,180.5)
1992	1,201,268	2,712,520.5	1,511,252.5	245,925	(1,265,327.5)	(9,687,508.0)
1993	1,390,981	2,207,692.5	816,711.5	282,533	(534,178.5)	(10,221,686.5)
1994	1,566,367	2,213,745.5	(647,378.5)	322,003	(325,375.5)	(10,547,062.0)

Note: Parentheses indicate shortfalls.

Table 4-11
Projected Operating Earnings for United Airlines Assuming Worst Case
(thousands of dollars)

Year	Internally Generated Funds	Total Capital Requirements	New Debt Required (Retired)	New Debt Possible	Surplus	Cumulative Surplus
1977-1979	522,446	1,179,777.0	657,331.0	—	(657,331.0)	(657,331.0)
1980	268,794	454,825.0	186,031.0	—	(186,031.0)	(843,362.0)
1981	299,178	561,274.0	262,096.0	—	(262,096.0)	(1,105,458.0)
1982	346,696	911,752.0	566,056.0	—	(566,056.0)	(1,670,514.0)
1983	409,654	1,055,681.0	646,027.0	48,815	(597,212.0)	(2,267,725.0)
1984	511,620	1,475,527.0	963,907.0	171,475	(792,432.0)	(3,060,157.0)
1985	639,066	1,784,961.0	1,145,895.0	194,299	(951,596.0)	(4,011,753.0)
1986	830,182	3,041,324.0	2,211,142.0	220,996	(1,990,146.0)	(6,001,899.0)
1987	1,037,193	2,502,078.0	1,464,885.0	163,516	(1,301,369.0)	(7,303,268.0)
1988	1,228,226	2,089,610.0	861,384.0	191,702	(669,682.0)	(7,972,950.0)
1989	1,420,587	2,135,103.0	714,516.0	223,047	(491,469.0)	(8,464,419.0)
1990	1,654,646	2,849,952.0	1,195,306.0	259,763	(935,543.0)	(9,399,962.0)
1991	1,908,221	2,828,358.5	920,137.5	294,697	(625,440.5)	(10,025,402.5)
1992	2,169,659	2,911,923.5	742,264.5	334,041	(408,223.5)	(10,433,626.0)
1993	2,439,157	3,456,586.5	1,017,429.5	379,467	(637,962.5)	(11,071,588.5)
1994	2,734,316	3,407,674.5	(673,358.5)	430,441	(242,917.5)	(11,314,506.0)

Note: Parentheses indicate shortfalls.

Table 4-12
Projected Operating Earnings for Western Airlines Assuming Worst Case
(thousands of dollars)

Year	Internally Generated Funds	Total Capital Requirements	New Debt Required (Retired)	New Debt Possible	Surplus	Cumulative Surplus
1977-
1979	157,810	158,279.5	469.5	3,148	2,678.5	2,678.5
1980	76,263	135,983.5	59,720.5	79,972	20,251.5	22,930.0
1981	90,350	135,115.0	44,765.0	71,700	26,935.0	49,865.0
1982	107,514	114,692.5	7,178.5	82,823	75,644.5	125,500.5
1983	122,356	193,013.0	70,657.0	95,407	24,750.0	150,259.5
1984	139,204	239,431.0	100,227.0	107,939	7,712.0	157,971.5
1985	173,081	268,866.0	95,785.0	123,203	27,418.0	185,389.5
1986	214,622	603,359.5	388,737.5	139,022	(249,715.5)	(64,326.0)
1987	262,919	581,645.0	318,726.0	144,027	(174,699.0)	(239,025.0)
1988	301,336	261,466.0	39,870.0	164,050	203,920.0	(35,105.0)
1989	332,614	300,183.5	(32,430.5)	186,599	219,029.5	183,924.5
1990	375,107	512,181.0	75,007.0	212,081	137,074.0	320,998.5
1991	436,492	696,560.5	260,068.5	240,941	(19,127.5)	301,871.0
1992	510,015	808,983.5	298,968.5	273,295	(25,673.5)	276,197.5
1993	589,559	730,304.5	140,745.0	310,733	169,988.0	446,185.5
1994	668,842	689,530.5	20,688.5	352,660	331,971.5	778,157.0

Note: Parentheses indicate shortfalls.

Table 4-13
Projected Operating Earnings for American Airlines Assuming Best Case
(thousands of dollars)

Year	Internally Generated Funds	Total Capital Requirements	New Debt Required (Retired)	New Debt Possible	Surplus	Cumulative Surplus
1977-1979	255,868	696,785.5	440,917.5	—	(440,917.5)	(440,917.5)
1980	134,371	294,609.5	160,238.5	212,458	52,309.5	(388,608.0)
1981	160,958	337,753.5	176,795.5	220,358	43,562.5	(345,045.5)
1982	168,374	624,947.0	456,573.0	244,549	(212,024.0)	(557,069.5)
1983	201,071	741,204.0	540,133.0	272,260	(267,873.0)	(824,942.5)
1984	236,743	861,243.5	624,500.5	301,957	(322,543.5)	(1,147,486.0)
1985	290,866	1,407,222.5	1,116,356.5	336,502	(779,854.5)	(1,927,340.5)
1986	348,187	1,772,734.5	1,424,547.5	481,424	(943,123.5)	(2,870,464.0)
1987	399,692	1,741,339.0	1,341,647.0	234,104	(1,107,543.0)	(3,978,007.0)
1988	448,971	1,403,629.0	954,658.0	289,646	(665,012.0)	(4,643,019.0)
1989	520,844	1,319,485.0	798,641.0	545,903	(252,738.0)	(4,895,757.0)
1990	602,354	2,487,137.5	1,884,783.5	576,749	(1,308,034.5)	(6,203,791.5)
1991	721,385	1,336,322.5	614,937.5	512,964	(101,973.5)	(6,305,765.0)
1992	352,084	1,534,201.0	1,182,117.0	661,345	(520,772.0)	(6,826,537.0)
1993	982,739	2,022,262.5	1,039,523.5	754,319	(285,204.5)	(7,111,741.5)
1994	1,129,864	2,449,131.5	1,319,267.5	857,214	(462,053.5)	(7,573,795.0)

Note: Parentheses indicate shortfalls.

Table 4-14
Projected Operating Earnings for Braniff International Corporation Assuming Best Case
(thousands of dollars)

Year	Internally Generated Funds	Total Capital Requirements	New Debt Required (Retired)	New Debt Possible	Surplus	Cumulative Surplus
1977-						
1979	224,529	144,733.5	(79,795.5)	33,473	113,268.5	113,268.5
1980	115,809	96,867.0	(18,942.0)	145,220	164,162.0	277,430.5
1981	145,872	110,936.0	(34,936.0)	137,704	172,640.0	450,070.5
1982	150,763	127,452.0	(23,311.0)	158,027	181,338.0	631,408.5
1983	180,459	146,061.5	(34,397.5)	181,230	215,627.5	847,036.0
1984	214,822	255,785.5	40,963.5	206,482	165,518.5	1,012,554.5
1985	267,069	593,336.5	326,269.5	234,984	(91,285.5)	921,269.0
1986	318,781	220,633.0	(98,148.0)	266,541	364,689.0	1,285,958.0
1987	372,064	348,594.5	(23,469.5)	284,188	307,657.5	1,593,615.5
1988	413,022	382,251.5	(30,770.5)	323,576	354,346.5	1,947,962.0
1989	475,370	490,007.5	14,637.5	368,190	353,552.5	2,301,515.0
1990	546,251	752,206.5	205,955.5	418,609	212,653.5	2,514,168.5
1991	653,648	1,195,586.5	541,938.0	475,478	(66,460.0)	2,447,708.5
1992	765,652	712,405.0	(53,247.0)	539,497	592,744.0	3,040,452.5
1993	876,287	893,594.0	17,307.0	613,378	596,071.0	3,636,523.5
1994	1,004,928	1,053,071.0	48,143.0	696,252	648,109.0	4,284,632.5

Note: Parentheses indicate shortfalls.

Table 4-15
Projected Operating Earnings for Continental Airlines Assuming Best Case
(thousands of dollars)

Year	Internally Generated Funds	Total Capital Requirements	New Debt Required (Retired)	New Debt Possible	Surplus	Cumulative Surplus
1977-1979	73,373	144,847.0	71,474.0	—	(71,474.0)	(71,474.0)
1980	91,992	204,547.5	112,555.5	—	(112,555.5)	(184,029.5)
1981	121,167	88,062.0	(33,105.0)	50,983	84,088.0	(99,941.5)
1982	134,420	101,116.0	(33,304.0)	94,290	127,594.0	27,652.5
1983	156,594	125,230.0	(31,364.0)	111,641	143,005.0	170,657.5
1984	182,096	132,825.5	(49,270.5)	131,491	180,761.5	351,419.0
1985	222,212	152,516.0	(69,696.0)	151,933	221,629.0	573,048.0
1986	250,261	485,271.5	235,010.5	173,943	(61,067.5)	511,980.5
1987	274,766	252,780.0	(21,986.0)	197,955	219,941.0	731,921.5
1988	321,820	381,273.0	59,453.0	237,292	177,839.0	909,760.5
1989	345,631	264,456.0	(81,175.0)	257,678	338,853.0	1,248,613.5
1990	403,891	745,615.0	341,724.0	293,172	(48,551.0)	1,200,062.5
1991	484,759	794,734.5	309,975.5	333,181	23,205.5	1,223,268.0
1992	574,963	824,039.0	249,076.0	378,807	129,731.0	1,352,999.0
1993	672,793	920,578.5	247,785.5	430,611	182,825.5	1,535,824.5
1994	767,884	607,892.5	(159,991.5)	488,454	648,445.5	2,184,270.0

Note: Parentheses indicate shortfalls.

Table 4-16
Projected Operating Earnings for Delta Airlines Assuming Best Case
(thousands of dollars)

Year	Internally Generated Funds	Total Capital Requirements	New Debt Required (Retired)	New Debt Possible	Surplus	Cumulative Surplus
1977- 1979	717,595	454,525.0	(263,070.0)	688,331	951,401.0	951,401.0
1980	320,566	323,358.0	2,792.	298,777	295,485.0	1,246,886.0
1981	421,041	292,005.5	(129,035.5)	318,998	448,033.5	1,694,919.5
1982	465,775	395,043.0	(70,732.0)	360,598	431,330.0	2,126,249.5
1983	522,683	449,161.0	(73,522.0)	408,412	481,934.0	2,608,183.5
1984	563,800	487,515.5	(76,284.5)	460,704	536,988.5	3,145,172.0
1985	606,976	760,244.5	153,268.5	520,365	367,096.5	3,512,268.5
1986	679,118	1,213,279.5	534,161.5	588,890	54,728.5	3,566,997.0
1987	746,041	1,220,518.0	474,477.0	643,984	169,507.0	3,736,504.0
1988	862,517	1,152,522.5	290,005.5	731,728	441,722.5	4,178,226.0
1989	995,170	968,571.5	(26,598.5)	831,180	857,778.5	5,036,005.0
1990	1,146,043	1,265,898.0	119,855.0	943,645	823,790.0	5,859,795.0
1991	1,317,429	2,339,861.5	1,022,432.5	1,070,554	48,121.5	5,907,916.5
1992	1,508,915	3,079,774.5	1,570,859.5	1,213,478	(357,381.5)	5,550,535.0
1993	1,735,963	2,456,605.0	720,642.0	1,378,505	657,863.0	6,208,398.0
1994	1,990,058	3,023,398.0	1,033,340.0	1,563,683	530,343.0	6,738,741.0

Note: Parentheses indicate shortfalls.

Table 4-17
Projected Operating Earnings for Eastern Airlines Assuming Best Case
(thousands of dollars)

Year	Internally Generated Funds	Total Capital Requirements	New Debt Required (Retired)	New Debt Possible	Surplus	Cumulative Surplus
1977-						
1979	216,121	554,402.0	338,281.0	—	(338,281.0)	(338,281.0)
1980	149,960	281,252.5	131,292.5	—	(131,292.5)	(469,573.5)
1981	237,648	352,041.0	114,393.0	59,081	(55,312.0)	(524,885.5)
1982	311,804	622,944.0	311,140.0	215,459	(95,681.0)	(620,566.6)
1983	342,700	644,176.5	301,476.5	256,095	(45,381.5)	(665,948.0)
1984	416,418	725,043.5	308,625.5	300,832	(7,793.5)	(673,741.5)
1985	499,983	965,842.0	465,859.0	340,190	(125,669.0)	(799,410.5)
1986	613,424	1,680,989.0	1,067,565.0	295,621	(771,944.0)	(1,571,354.5)
1987	734,224	1,138,874.0	404,650.0	384,637	(20,013.0)	(1,591,367.5)
1988	825,057	968,519.0	143,462.0	439,304	295,842.0	(1,295,525.5)
1989	944,872	1,329,020.5	384,148.5	500,756	116,607.5	(1,178,918.0)
1990	1,100,709	1,996,133.5	895,424.5	570,892	(324,532.5)	(1,503,450.5)
1991	1,321,569	3,168,111.5	1,846,542.5	697,543	(1,148,999.5)	(2,652,450.0)
1992	1,553,860	1,719,330.5	165,470.5	728,415	562,944.5	(2,089,505.5)
1993	1,760,803	2,101,122.5	340,319.5	841,404	501,084.5	(1,588,421.0)
1994	1,939,374	1,514,828.0	(424,546.0)	955,187	1,379,733.0	(208,688.0)

Note: Parentheses indicate shortfalls.

Table 4-18
Projected Operating Earnings for National Airlines Assuming Best Case
(thousands of dollars)

Year	Internally Generated Funds	Total Capital Requirements	New Debt Required (Retired)	New Debt Possible	Surplus	Cumulative Surplus
1977-						
1979	199,706	121,676.5	(78,029.5)	190,813	268,842.5	268,842.5
1980	87,010	81,348.0	(5,662.0)	70,520	76,182.0	345,024.5
1981	100,548	93,282.5	(7,265.5)	64,968	71,963.5	416,988.0
1982	118,151	170,355.0	52,204.0	77,903	25,699.0	442,687.0
1983	141,255	247,335.0	106,080.0	111,137	5,057.0	447,744.0
1984	165,620	196,425.5	30,805.5	124,334	93,528.5	541,272.5
1985	191,165	237,839.0	46,674.0	139,457	92,783.0	634,055.5
1986	233,284	761,820.0	528,536.0	156,738	(371,798.0)	262,257.5
1987	269,700	212,885.0	(56,815.0)	163,761	220,576.0	482,833.5
1988	298,817	244,043.0	(54,774.0)	186,073	240,847.0	723,680.5
1989	342,741	486,193.0	143,452.0	211,364	67,912.0	791,592.5
1990	398,619	766,349.5	367,730.5	239,963	(127,767.5)	663,825.0
1991	465,809	538,770.0	72,961.0	272,235	199,274.0	863,099.0
1992	525,627	423,791.5	(101,836.0)	308,582	410,418.0	1,273,517.0
1993	600,419	870,934.0	(270,515.0)	350,543	80,028.0	1,353,545.0
1994	683,622	558,574.0	(125,048.0)	397,637	522,685.0	1,876,230.0

Note: Parentheses indicate shortfalls.

Table 4-19
Projected Operating Earnings for Northwest Airlines Assuming Best Case
(thousands of dollars).

Year	Internally Generated Funds	Total Capital Requirements	New Debt Required (Retired)	New Debt Possible	Surplus	Cumulative Surplus
1977-1979	627,071	269,470.0	(357,601.0)	1,053,364	1,410,965.0	1,410,965.0
1980	276,583	175,735.5	(100,847.5)	220,518	321,365.0	1,732,330.5
1981	307,262	206,691.0	(100,571.0)	238,768	339,339.0	2,071,669.5
1982	352,704	278,496.5	(74,207.5)	272,053	346,260.5	2,417,930.0
1983	408,073	435,861.0	27,788.0	314,143	286,355.0	2,704,285.5
1984	464,988	472,978.5	7,990.5	354,848	346,857.5	3,051,143.0
1985	507,944	462,221.0	(45,723.0)	401,495	447,218.0	3,498,361.0
1986	579,767	921,390.0	341,623.0	454,782	113,159.0	3,611,520.0
1987	688,747	889,908.5	201,161.5	505,082	303,920.5	3,915,440.5
1988	793,159	1,409,633.5	616,474.5	573,898	(42,576.5)	3,872,864.0
1989	924,640	1,089,865.5	165,225.5	651,899	486,673.5	4,359,537.5
1990	1,046,972	712,385.0	(334,587.0)	740,106	1,074,693.0	5,434,230.5
1991	1,203,122	1,867,677.5	664,555.5	839,640	175,084.5	5,609,315.0
1992	1,399,085	1,467,894.0	68,809.0	951,737	882,928.0	6,492,243.0
1993	1,595,601	1,431,895.5	(163,705.5)	1,081,167	1,244,872.5	7,737,115.5
1994	1,806,465	1,513,193.0	(293,272.0)	1,226,403	1,519,675.0	9,256,790.5

Note: Parentheses indicate shortfalls.

Table 4-20

Projected Operating Earnings for Pan American World Airways Assuming Best Case

(thousands of dollars)

Year	Internally Generated Funds	Total Capital Requirements	New Debt Required (Retired)	New Debt Possible	Surplus	Cumulative Surplus
1977-						
1979	115,833	338,859.0	223,026.0	—	(223,026.0)	(223,026.0)
1980	73,603	226,681.0	153,078.0	—	(153,078.0)	(376,104.0)
1981	88,084	259,858.0	171,774.0	—	(171,774.0)	(547,878.0)
1982	105,248	381,319.0	276,071.0	—	(276,071.0)	(823,949.0)
1983	131,868	641,693.5	509,825.5	—	(509,825.5)	(1,333,774.5)
1984	172,995	709,121.5	536,126.5	—	(536,126.5)	(1,869,901.0)
1985	222,034	1,152,842.5	930,808.5	—	(930,808.5)	(2,800,709.5)
1986	275,323	970,341.0	695,018.0	—	(695,018.0)	(3,495,727.5)
1987	351,051	1,158,167.5	807,116.5	—	(807,116.5)	(4,302,844.0)
1988	477,974	2,469,860.0	1,991,886.0	—	(1,991,886.0)	(6,294,730.0)
1989	613,051	1,332,708.0	719,657.0		(719,657.0)	(7,014,387.0)
1990	710,825	895,699.5	184,874.5	8,539	(176,335.5)	(7,190,722.5)
1991	806,109	1,144,673.5	338,564.5	142,901	(195,663.5)	(7,386,386.0)
1992	890,900	1,180,241.0	289,341.0	164,028	(125,313.0)	(7,511,699.0)
1993	988,818	1,355,094.0	366,276.0	187,598	(178,678.0)	(7,690,377.0)
1994	1,123,632	2,232,053.5	1,108,421.5	214,597	(893,824.5)	(8,584,201.5)

Note: Parentheses indicate shortfalls.

Table 4-21
Projected Operating Earnings for Trans World Airlines Assuming Best Case
(thousands of dollars)

Year	Internally Generated Funds	Total Capital Requirements	New Debt Required (Retired)	New Debt Possible	Surplus	Cumulative Surplus
1977-1979	—	629,090.5	629,090.5	—	(629,090.5)	(629,090.5)
1980	138,090	528,859.0	390,769.0	—	(390,769.0)	(1,019,859.5)
1981	200,036	347,233.0	147,197.0	—	(147,197.0)	(1,167,056.5)
1982	268,681	618,938.0	350,257.0	—	(350,257.0)	(1,517,313.5)
1983	325,902	647,462.0	321,560.0	—	(321,560.0)	(1,838,873.5)
1984	399,444	1,099,030.5	699,586.5	—	(699,586.5)	(2,538,460.0)
1985	485,783	1,130,320.0	644,537.0	243,916	(400,621.0)	(2,939,081.0)
1986	594,973	1,289,784.5	694,811.5	292,551	(402,260.5)	(3,341,341.5)
1987	664,625	1,492,591.5	827,966.5	260,475	(567,491.5)	(3,908,833.0)
1988	794,362	1,783,291.0	988,929.0	300,377	(688,552.0)	(4,597,385.0)
1989	948,883	1,513,122.5	564,239.5	344,494	(219,745.5)	(4,817,130.5)
1990	1,064,639	1,759,816.5	695,177.5	394,970	(300,207.5)	(5,117,338.0)
1991	1,219,275	1,979,940.0	760,665.0	450,830	(309,835.0)	(5,427,173.0)
1992	1,421,459	2,712,520.5	1,291,061.5	515,047	(776,014.5)	(6,203,187.5)
1993	1,641,117	2,207,692.5	566,575.5	588,255	21,679.5	(6,181,508.0)
1994	1,850,105	2,213,745.5	363,640.5	668,794	305,153.5	(5,876,354.5)

Note: Parentheses indicate shortfalls.

Table 4-22
Projected Operating Earnings for United Airlines Assuming Best Case
(thousands of dollars)

Year	Internally Generated Funds	Total Capital Requirements	New Debt Required (Retired)	New Debt Possible	Surplus	Cumulative Surplus
1977-						
1979	602,092	1,179,777.0	577,685.0	—	(577,685.0)	(577,685.0)
1980	303,067	454,825.0	151,758.0	—	(151,758.0)	(729,443.0)
1981	338,019	561,274.0	223,255.0		(223,255.0)	(962,698.0)
1982	390,829	911,752.0	520,923.0	128,026	(392,897.0)	(1,345,595.0)
1983	459,891	1,055,681.0	595,790.0	210,615	(385,175.0)	(1,730,770.0)
1984	568,536	1,475,527.0	906,991.0	240,949	(666,042.0)	(2,396,812.0)
1985	703,635	1,784,961.0	1,081,326.0	273,306	(808,020.0)	(3,204,832.0)
1986	903,498	3,041,324.0	2,137,826.0	310,604	(1,827,222.0)	(5,032,054.0)
1987	1,120,076	2,502,078.0	1,382,002.0	264,818	(1,117,184.0)	(6,149,238.0)
1988	1,322,399	2,089,610.0	767,211.0	306,803	(460,408.0)	(6,609,646.0)
1989	1,527,562	2,135,103.0	607,541.0	353,794	(253,747.0)	(6,863,393.0)
1990	1,776,091	2,849,952.0	1,073,861.0	408,195	(665,666.0)	(7,529,059.0)
1991	2,046,001	2,828,358.5	782,357.5	463,095	(319,262.5)	(7,848,321.5)
1992	2,325,835	2,911,923.5	586,088.5	524,923	(61,165.5)	(7,909,487.0)
1993	2,616,572	3,456,586.5	840,014.5	596,307	(243,707.5)	(8,153,194.5)
1994	2,935,565	3,407,674.5	472,109.5	676,412	204,302.5	(7,948,892.0)

Note: Parentheses indicate shortfalls.

Table 4-23
Projected Operating Earnings for Western Airlines Assuming Best Case
(thousands of dollars)

Year	Internally Generated Funds	Total Capital Requirements	New Debt Required (Retired)	New Debt Possible	Surplus	Cumulative Surplus
1977-						
1979	178,784	158,279.5	(20,504.5)	28,783	49,287.5	49,287.5
1980	85,289	135,983.5	50,694.5	91,003	40,308.5	89,596.0
1981	100,578	135,115.0	34,537.0	84,201	49,664.0	139,260.0
1982	119,137	114,692.5	(4,444.5)	97,029	101,473.5	240,733.5
1983	135,586	193,013.0	57,427.0	111,578	54,151.0	294,884.5
1984	154,193	239,431.0	85,238.0	126,258	41,020.0	335,904.5
1985	190,084	268,866.0	78,782.0	143,655	64,873.0	400,777.5
1986	233,928	603,359.5	369,431.5	162,948	(206,483.5)	194,294.0
1987	284,771	581,645.0	296,874.0	170,702	(126,172.0)	68,122.0
1988	326,137	261,466.0	(64,671.0)	194,362	259,033.0	327,155.0
1989	360,784	300,183.5	(60,600.5)	221,029	281,629.5	608,784.5
1990	407,091	512,181.0	105,090.0	251,173	146,083.0	754,867.5
1991	472,775	696,560.5	223,785.5	285,287	61,501.5	816,369.0
1992	551,144	808,983.5	257,839.5	323,564	65,724.5	882,093.5
1993	636,279	730,304.5	94,025.5	367,834	273,808.5	1,155,902.0
1994	721,841	689,530.5	32,310.5	417,437	449,747.5	1,605,649.5

Note: Parentheses indicate shortfalls.

It is now possible to state by company and year the amount of feasible new debt under the alternative earnings assumptions. Possible new debt appears in tables 4-24—4-44.

Taking into account interest charges on new debt possible and required, the study now arrives at the shortage or surplus by company for each year and cumulatively through time. Tables 4-45 to 4-55 accomplish this, and present in summary form the findings of this study. The following is a company-by-company analysis of the findings.

American Airlines

American Airlines earned more in 1976 than in any prior year.[1] Earnings of $56.3 million represented a $78.7 million turnaround from 1975's $22.4 million loss.[2] However, the truth is that the apparently improved performance—even if sustained indefinitely—is far from adequate. American's 1976 operating ratio was .964, better than any year since 1969 when it was .952. To finance capital needs, a consistent operating ratio of .939 would have to be maintained. In 1977 American was the beneficiary of unusually favorable fuel prices. Contracts that did not expire until late in the year allowed the company to purchase fuel almost four cents a gallon less than the industry.[3] This savings translates into approximately $50 million, or 61 percent of the company's record-breaking 1977 profits of $81.9 million. Yet even this windfall only represents an operating ratio of .972 (interest income contributed $30.6 million and this is nonoperating income).

If American can maintain its 1976 operating ratio—a reasonable assumption—a capital shortfall of $2.4 billion by the end of 1985 and $6.3 billion by 1990 is indicated. If the corporation fails to improve on its performance for the five years ended December 31, 1976, the shortage will be $3.6 billion by the end of 1985 and $7.4 billion by the end of the decade. If American were to succeed in maintaining its rather leveraged capital structure, it could reduce the shortfall as follows:

Period ending December 31, 1985

Best case	$1.2 billion
Worst case	$3.1 billion

Period ending December 31, 1989

Best case	$4.2 billion
Worst case	$6.7 billion

This demonstrates that additional earnings—not leverage alone—is the key to

Table 4-24

New Debt Estimates for American Airlines with Five-Year Operating Ratio of .989

(thousands of dollars)

Year	Operating Revenues (1976 Dollars)	Operating Expenses (1976 Dollars)	Operating Earnings (1976 Dollars)	Inflation Factor (7 Percent)	Operating Earnings (Current Dollars)
1977-					
1979	6,782,352	6,705,033	77,319	1.14	88,143
1980	2,539,692	2,510,740	28,952	1.31	37,928
1981	2,693,343	2,662,639	30,704	1.40	42,986
1982	2,856,290	2,823,728	32,562	1.50	48,843
1983	3,029,096	2,994,564	34,532	1.61	55,597
1984	3,212,356	3,175,735	36,621	1.72	62,988
1985	3,406,704	3,367,868	38,836	1.84	71,458
1986	3,612,810	3,571,624	41,186	1.97	81,136
1987	3,831,385	3,787,707	43,678	2.10	91,724
1988	4,063,184	4,016,864	46,320	2.25	104,220
1989	4,309,007	4,259,884	49,123	2.41	118,386
1990	4,569,702	4,517,607	52,095	2.58	134,405
1991	4,846,169	4,790,923	55,246	2.76	152,479
1992	5,139,362	5,080,773	58,589	2.95	172,838
1993	5,450,293	5,388,160	62,133	3.16	196,340
1994	5,780,036	5,714,444	65,892	3.38	222,715

financing the industry's capital needs. American's shortage for the 1980s under the worst case assumption was only reduced from $7.4 billion to $6.7 billion by extending the debt-to-equity ratio from our assumed level of 55/45 to the December 31, 1976 level of 66/34. With higher earnings, the increased leverage (be it in the form of conventional debt or capital leases) reduces the December 31, 1985 cumulative shortfall from $2.4 billion to $1.2 billion, and the shortage through 1989 from $6.3 billion to $4.2 billion.

Another qualification to 1977 earnings must be noted. Because of a revision to the tax law, airlines received a favorable treatment with respect to extending carry-forwards on the investment tax credit. Pretax and before the subsidiary effect, 1977 earnings were only $1.03 million higher, even counting the high interest income earned in 1977.

One factor that must be worked out if American is to overcome its earnings hurdle is the disposition of its Americana Hotel Chain. Held under a long-term, noncancellable lease with the Loew's Corporation, the enterprise has proved to be nothing short of disastrous for American. Americana Hotels have never shown a profit since the airline acquired the business in 1972. The 1976 loss was $11.9 million. For the four years ended December 31, 1976, the loss was $27.8 million.[4]

Table 4-25
New Debt Estimates for Braniff International Corporation with Five-Year
Operating Ratio of .913
(thousands of dollars)

Year	Operating Revenues (1976 Dollars)	Operating Expenses (1976 Dollars)	Operating Earnings (1976 Dollars)	Inflation Factor (7 Percent)	Operating Earnings (Current Dollars)
1977-					
1979	2,278,647	2,080,405	198,242	1.14	225,996
1980	853,253	779,020	74,233	1.31	97,245
1981	904,875	826,151	78,724	1.40	110,214
1982	959,620	876,133	83,487	1.50	125,231
1983	1,017,677	929,139	88,538	1.61	142,546
1984	1,079,246	985,352	93,894	1.72	161,498
1985	1,144,540	1,044,965	99,575	1.84	183,218
1986	1,213,785	1,108,186	105,599	1.97	208,030
1987	1,287,219	1,175,231	111,988	2.10	235,175
1988	1,365,096	1,246,333	118,763	2.25	267,217
1989	1,447,684	1,321,735	125,949	2.41	303,537
1990	1,535,269	1,401,701	133,568	2.58	344,605
1991	1,628,153	1,486,504	141,649	2.76	390,951
1992	1,726,656	1,576,437	150,219	2.95	443,146
1993	1,831,119	1,671,812	159,307	3.16	503,410
1994	1,941,902	1,772,957	168,945	3.38	571,034

The corporation devoted a large section of its most recent annual report to financing the large capital needs imposed by noise and air pollution legislation, as well as economic obsolescence:

> To be sure, the prospect of having to make capital expenditures to improve the environment at the expense of the balance sheet is not unique to the airlines. But the enormity of the cost . . . has given rise to concern as to whether it is equitable—or even practicable—to expect the airlines to bear this burden without some additional provisions designed to facilitate capital formation.[5]

Shareholders' equity actually declined from $604.2 million on December 31, 1972 to $553.2 million on December 31, 1975, but recovered to $610.1 million by December 31, 1976. Retained earnings stood lower on December 31, 1976 than on December 31, 1968 ($263.9 million as opposed to $272.3 million).[6]

American's wage and benefits expenses rose 12.4 percent in 1976 over 1975, with only 3.1 percent additional employees. Wage and benefits expenses had risen by 91.5 percent between 1969 and 1976, even though fewer people were employed at year end 1976 than at year end 1969 (35,984 at year end

Table 4-26
New Debt Estimates for Continental Airlines with Five-Year Operating Ratio of .924
(thousands of dollars)

Year	Operating Revenues (1976 Dollars)	Operating Expenses (1976 Dollars)	Operating Earnings (1976 Dollars)	Inflation Factor (7 Percent)	Operating Earnings (Current Dollars)
1977-1979	1,825,546	1,686,805	138,741	1.14	158,165
1980	683,587	631,634	51,953	1.31	68,058
1981	724,944	669,848	55,096	1.40	77,134
1982	768,803	710,374	58,429	1.50	87,644
1983	815,316	753,352	61,964	1.61	99,762
1984	864,643	798,930	65,713	1.72	113,026
1985	916,954	847,265	69,689	1.84	128,228
1986	972,430	898,525	73,905	1.97	145,593
1987	1,031,262	952,886	78,376	2.10	164,590
1988	1,093,653	1,010,535	87,118	2.25	196,016
1989	1,159,819	1,071,673	88,146	2.41	212,432
1990	1,229,988	1,136,509	93,479	2.58	241,176
1991	1,304,402	1,205,267	99,135	2.76	273,613
1992	1,383,318	1,278,186	105,132	2.95	310,139
1993	1,467,009	1,355,516	111,493	3.16	352,318
1994	1,555,763	1,437,525	118,238	3.38	399,644

Table 4-27
New Debt Estimates for Delta Airlines with Five-Year Operating Ratio of .914
(thousands of dollars)

Year	Operating Revenues (1976 Dollars)	Operating Expenses (1976 Dollars)	Operating Earnings (1976 Dollars)	Inflation Factor (7 Percent)	Operating Earnings (Current Dollars)
1977-1979	5,164,555	4,720,403	444,152	1.14	506,333
1980	1,933,898	1,767,583	166,315	1.31	217,873
1981	2,050,899	1,874,522	176,377	1.40	246,928
1982	2,174,978	1,987,930	187,048	1.50	280,572
1983	2,306,564	2,108,199	198,365	1.61	319,368
1984	2,446,111	2,235,745	210,366	1.72	361,830
1985	2,594,101	2,371,008	223,093	1.84	410,491
1986	2,751,044	2,514,454	236,590	1.97	466,082
1987	2,917,482	2,666,579	250,903	2.10	526,896
1988	3,093,990	2,827,907	266,083	2.25	598,687
1989	3,281,176	2,998,995	282,181	2.41	680,056
1990	3,479,687	3,180,434	299,253	2.58	772,073
1991	3,690,208	3,372,850	317,358	2.76	875,908
1992	3,913,466	3,576,908	336,558	2.95	992,846
1993	4,150,231	3,793,311	356,920	3.16	1,127,867
1994	4,401,320	4,022,806	378,514	3.38	1,279,377

Table 4-28
New Debt Estimates for Eastern Airlines with Five-Year Operating Ratio of .975
(thousands of dollars)

Year	Operating Revenues (1976 Dollars)	Operating Expenses (1976 Dollars)	Operating Earnings (1976 Dollars)	Inflation Factor (7 Percent)	Operating Earnings (Current Dollars)
1977-					
1979	6,166,203	6,012,048	154,155	1.14	175,737
1980	2,308,972	2,251,248	57,724	1.31	75,618
1981	2,448,665	2,387,448	61,217	1.40	85,704
1982	2,596,809	2,531,889	64,920	1.50	97,380
1983	2,753,916	2,685,068	68,848	1.61	110,845
1984	2,920,528	2,847,515	73,013	1.72	125,582
1985	3,097,220	3,019,790	77,430	1.84	142,471
1986	3,284,602	3,202,487	82,115	1.97	161,767
1987	3,483,320	3,396,237	87,083	2.10	182,874
1988	3,694,061	3,601,709	92,352	2.25	207,792
1989	3,917,552	3,819,613	97,939	2.41	236,033
1990	4,154,564	4,050,700	103,864	2.58	267,939
1991	4,405,915	4,295,767	110,148	2.76	304,008
1992	4,672,473	4,555,661	116,812	2.95	344,595
1993	4,955,158	4,831,279	123,879	3.16	391,458
1994	5,254,945	5,123,571	131,374	3.38	444,044

Table 4-29
New Debt Estimates for National Airlines with Five-Year Operating Ratio of .900
(thousands of dollars)

Year	Operating Revenues (1976 Dollars)	Operating Expenses (1976 Dollars)	Operating Earnings (1976 Dollars)	Inflation Factor (7 Percent)	Operating Earnings (Current Dollars)
1977-					
1979	1,129,451	1,016,506	112,945	1.14	128,757
1980	422,930	380,637	42,293	1.31	55,404
1981	448,517	403,665	44,852	1.40	62,793
1982	475,652	428,087	47,565	1.50	71,348
1983	504,429	453,986	50,443	1.61	81,213
1984	534,947	481,452	53,495	1.72	92,011
1985	567,311	510,580	56,731	1.84	104,385
1986	601,633	541,470	60,163	1.97	118,521
1987	638,032	574,229	63,803	2.10	133,986
1988	676,633	608,970	67,663	2.25	152,242
1989	717,569	645,812	71,757	2.41	172,934
1990	760,982	684,884	76,098	2.58	196,333
1991	807,021	726,319	80,702	2.76	222,738
1992	855,846	770,261	85,585	2.95	252,476
1993	907,625	816,863	90,762	3.16	286,808
1994	962,536	866,282	96,254	3.38	325,339

Table 4-30
New Debt Estimates for Northwest Airlines with Five-Year Operating Ratio of .915
(thousands of dollars)

Year	Operating Revenues (1976 Dollars)	Operating Expenses (1976 Dollars)	Operating Earnings (1976 Dollars)	Inflation Factor (7 Percent)	Operating Earnings (Current Dollars)
1977-1979	3,255,609	2,978,882	276,727	1.14	315,469
1980	1,219,082	1,115,460	103,622	1.31	135,745
1981	1,292,836	1,182,945	109,891	1.40	153,847
1982	1,371,053	1,254,513	116,540	1.50	174,810
1983	1,454,002	1,330,412	123,590	1.61	198,980
1984	1,541,969	1,410,902	131,067	1.72	225,435
1985	1,635,258	1,496,261	138,997	1.84	255,754
1986	1,734,191	1,586,785	147,406	1.97	290,390
1987	1,839,110	1,682,786	156,324	2.10	328,280
1988	1,950,376	1,784,594	165,782	2.25	373,010
1989	2,068,374	1,892,562	175,812	2.41	423,707
1990	2,193,511	2,007,063	186,448	2.58	481,036
1991	2,326,218	2,128,489	197,729	2.76	545,732
1992	2,466,954	2,257,263	209,691	2.95	618,588
1993	2,616,205	2,393,828	222,377	3.16	702,711
1994	2,774,485	2,538,654	235,831	3.38	797,109

Table 4-31
New Debt Estimates for Trans World Airlines with Five-Year Operating Ratio of .987
(thousands of dollars)

Year	Operating Revenues (1976 Dollars)	Operating Expenses (1976 Dollars)	Operating Earnings (1976 Dollars)	Inflation Factor (7 Percent)	Operating Earnings (Current Dollars)
1977-1979	7,035,567	6,944,105	91,462	1.14	104,267
1980	2,634,510	2,600,261	34,249	1.31	44,866
1981	2,793,898	2,757,577	36,321	1.40	50,849
1982	2,962,929	2,924,411	38,518	1.50	57,777
1983	3,142,186	3,101,338	40,848	1.61	65,765
1984	3,332,288	3,288,968	43,320	1.72	74,510
1985	3,533,892	3,487,951	45,941	1.84	84,531
1986	3,747,692	3,698,972	48,720	1.97	95,978
1987	3,974,427	3,922,759	51,668	2.10	108,503
1988	4,214,880	4,160,087	54,793	2.25	132,284
1989	4,469,880	4,411,772	58,108	2.41	140,040
1990	4,740,308	4,678,684	61,624	2.58	158,990
1991	5,027,097	4,961,745	65,352	2.76	180,372
1992	5,331,236	5,261,930	69,306	2.95	204,453
1993	5,653,776	5,580,277	73,499	3.16	232,257
1994	5,995,829	5,917,883	77,946	3.38	263,457

Table 4-32
New Debt Estimates for United Airlines with Five-Year Operating Ratio of .978
(thousands of dollars)

Year	Operating Revenues (1976 Dollars)	Operating Expenses (1976 Dollars)	Operating Earnings (1976 Dollars)	Inflation Factor (7 Percent)	Operating Earnings (Current Dollars)
1977-					
1979	8,733,133	8,541,004	192,129	1.14	219,027
1980	3,270,174	3,198,230	71,944	1.31	94,247
1981	3,468,020	3,391,724	76,296	1.40	106,814
1982	3,677,835	3,596,923	80,912	1.50	121,368
1983	3,900,344	3,814,536	85,808	1.61	138,151
1984	4,136,315	4,045,316	90,999	1.72	156,518
1985	4,386,562	4,290,058	96,504	1.84	177,567
1986	4,651,949	4,549,606	102,343	1.07	201,616
1987	4,933,392	4,824,857	108,535	2.10	227,924
1988	5,231,862	5,116,761	115,101	2.25	258,977
1989	5,548,390	5,426,325	122,065	2.41	294,177
1990	5,884,068	5,754,619	129,449	2.58	333,978
1991	6,240,054	6,102,773	137,281	2.76	378,896
1992	6,617,577	6,471,990	145,587	2.95	429,482
1993	7,017,940	6,863,545	154,395	3.16	487,888
1994	7,442,525	7,278,789	163,736	3.38	553,428

Table 4-33
New Debt Estimates for Western Airlines with Five-Year Operating Ratio of .942
(thousands of dollars)

Year	Operating Revenues (1976 Dollars)	Operating Expenses (1976 Dollars)	Operating Earnings (1976 Dollars)	Inflation Factor (7 Percent)	Operating Earnings (Current Dollars)
1977-					
1979	2,044,299	1,925,730	118,569	1.14	135,169
1980	765,500	721,101	44,399	1.31	58,163
1981	811,813	764,728	47,085	1.40	65,919
1982	860,928	810,994	49,934	1.50	74,901
1983	913,014	860,059	52,955	1.61	85,258
1984	968,251	912,092	56,159	1.72	96,593
1985	1,026,830	967,274	59,556	1.84	109,583
1986	1,088,953	1,025,794	63,159	1.97	124,423
1987	1,154,835	1,087,855	66,980	2.10	140,658
1988	1,224,703	1,153,670	71,033	2.25	159,824
1989	1,298,798	1,223,468	75,330	2.41	181,545
1990	1,377,375	1,297,487	79,888	2.58	206,111
1991	1,460,706	1,375,985	84,721	2.76	233,830
1992	1,549,079	1,459,232	89,847	2.95	265,049
1993	1,642,798	1,547,576	95,282	3.16	301,091
1994	1,742,187	1,641,140	101,047	3.38	341,539

Table 4-34
New Debt Estimates for American Airlines with 1976 Operating Ratio
of .964
(thousands of dollars)

Year	Operating Revenues (1976 Dollars)	Operating Expenses (1976 Dollars)	Operating Earnings (1976 Dollars)	Inflation Factor (7 Percent)	Operating Earnings (Current Dollars)
1977-1979	6,782,352	6,538,187	244,165	1.14	278,348
1980	2,539,692	2,448,263	91,429	1.31	119,772
1981	2,693,343	2,596,383	96,960	1.40	135,744
1982	2,856,290	2,753,464	102,826	1.50	154,239
1983	3,029,096	2,920,049	109,047	1.61	175,566
1984	3,212,356	3,096,711	115,645	1.72	198,909
1985	3,406,704	3,284,063	122,641	1.84	225,659
1986	3,612,810	3,482,749	130,061	1.97	256,220
1987	3,831,385	3,693,455	137,930	2.10	289,653
1988	4,063,184	3,916,909	146,275	2.25	329,119
1989	4,309,007	4,153,883	155,124	2.41	373,849
1990	4,569,702	4,405,193	164,509	2.58	424,433
1991	4,846,169	4,671,707	174,462	2.76	481,515
1992	5,139,362	4,954,345	185,017	2.95	545,800
1993	5,450,293	5,254,082	196,211	3.16	620,027
1994	5,780,036	5,571,955	208,081	3.38	703,314

Table 4-35
New Debt Estimates for Braniff International Corporation with 1976 Operating
Ratio of .922
(thousands of dollars)

Year	Operating Revenues (1976 Dollars)	Operating Expenses (1976 Dollars)	Operating Earnings (1976 Dollars)	Inflation Factor (7 Percent)	Operating Earnings (Current Dollars)
1977-1979	2,278,647	2,100,913	177,734	1.14	202,617
1980	853,253	786,699	66,554	1.31	87,186
1981	904,875	834,295	70,580	1.40	98,812
1982	959,620	884,770	74,850	1.50	112,275
1983	1,017,677	938,298	79,379	1.61	127,800
1984	1,079,246	995,065	84,181	1.72	144,791
1985	1,144,540	1,055,266	89,274	1.84	164,264
1986	1,213,785	1,119,110	94,675	1.97	186,510
1987	1,287,219	1,186,816	100,403	2.10	210,846
1988	1,365,096	1,258,619	106,477	2.25	239,573
1989	1,447,684	1,334,765	122,919	2.41	296,235
1990	1,535,269	1,415,518	119,751	2.58	308,958
1991	1,628,153	1,501,157	126,996	2.76	350,509
1992	1,726,656	1,591,977	134,679	2.95	397,303
1993	1,831,119	1,688,292	142,827	3.16	451,333
1994	1,941,902	1,790,434	151,468	3.38	511,962

Table 4-36
New Debt Estimates for Continental Airlines with 1976 Operating Ratio of .943
(thousands of dollars)

Year	Operating Revenues (1976 Dollars)	Operating Expenses (1976 Dollars)	Operating Earnings (1976 Dollars)	Inflation Factor (7 Percent)	Operating Earnings (Current Dollars)
1977-
1979	1,825,546	1,721,490	104,056	1.14	118,624
1980	683,587	644,623	38,964	1.31	51,043
1981	724,944	683,622	41,322	1.40	57,851
1982	768,803	724,981	43,822	1.50	65,733
1983	815,316	768,843	46,473	1.61	74,822
1984	864,643	815,358	49,285	1.72	84,770
1985	916,954	864,688	51,966	1.84	95,617
1986	972,430	917,001	55,429	1.97	109,195
1987	1,031,262	972,480	58,782	2.10	123,442
1988	1,093,653	1,031,315	62,338	2.25	140,261
1989	1,159,819	1,093,709	66,110	2.41	159,325
1990	1,229,988	1,159,879	70,109	2.58	180,881
1991	1,304,402	1,230,051	74,351	2.76	205,209
1992	1,383,318	1,304,469	78,849	2.95	232,605
1993	1,467,009	1,383,389	83,620	3.16	264,239
1994	1,555,763	1,467,085	88,678	3.38	299,732

Table 4-37
New Debt Estimates for Delta Airlines with 1976 Operating Ratio of .923
(thousands of dollars)

Year	Operating Revenues (1976 Dollars)	Operating Expenses (1976 Dollars)	Operating Earnings (1976 Dollars)	Inflation Factor (7 Percent)	Operating Earnings (Current Dollars)
1977-
1979	5,164,555	4,766,884	397,671	1.14	453,345
1980	1,933,898	1,784,988	148,910	1.31	195,072
1981	2,050,899	1,892,980	157,919	1.40	221,087
1982	2,174,978	2,007,505	167,473	1.50	251,210
1983	2,306,564	2,128,959	177,605	1.61	285,944
1984	2,446,111	2,257,760	188,351	1.72	323,964
1985	2,594,101	2,394,355	199,746	1.84	367,533
1986	2,751,044	2,539,214	211,830	1.97	417,305
1987	2,917,482	2,692,836	224,646	2.10	471,757
1988	3,093,990	2,855,753	238,237	2.25	536,033
1989	3,281,176	3,028,525	252,651	2.41	608,889
1990	3,479,687	3,211,751	267,936	2.58	691,275
1991	3,690,208	3,406,062	284,146	2.76	784,243
1992	3,913,466	3,612,129	301,337	2.95	888,944
1993	4,150,231	3,830,663	319,568	3.16	1,009,835
1994	4,401,320	4,062,418	338,902	3.38	1,145,489

Table 4-38
New Debt Estimates for Eastern Airlines with 1976 Operating Ratio of .956
(thousands of dollars)

Year	Operating Revenues (1976 Dollars)	Operating Expenses (1976 Dollars)	Operating Earnings (1976 Dollars)	Inflation Factor (7 Percent)	Operating Earnings (Current Dollars)
1977-1979	6,166,203	5,894,890	271,313	1.14	309,297
1980	2,308,972	2,207,377	101,595	1.31	133,089
1981	2,448,665	2,340,924	107,741	1.40	150,837
1982	2,596,809	2,482,549	114,260	1.50	171,390
1983	2,753,916	2,632,744	121,172	1.61	195,087
1984	2,920,528	2,792,025	128,503	1.72	221,025
1985	3,097,220	2,960,942	136,278	1.84	251,580
1986	3,284,602	3,140,080	144,522	1.97	284,708
1987	3,483,320	3,330,054	153,266	2.10	321,859
1988	3,694,061	3,531,522	162,539	2.25	365,713
1989	3,917,552	3,745,180	172,372	2.41	415,417
1990	4,154,564	3,971,763	182,801	2.58	471,627
1991	4,405,915	4,212,055	193,860	2.76	535,054
1992	4,672,473	4,466,884	205,589	2.95	606,488
1993	4,955,158	4,737,131	218,027	3.16	688,965
1994	5,254,945	5,023,727	231,218	3.38	781,517

Table 4-39
New Debt Estimates for National Airlines with 1976 Operating Ratio of .973
(thousands of dollars)

Year	Operating Revenues (1976 Dollars)	Operating Expenses (1976 Dollars)	Operating Earnings (1976 Dollars)	Inflation Factor (7 Percent)	Operating Earnings (Current Dollars)
1977-1979	1,129,451	1,098,956	30,495	1.14	34,764
1980	422,930	411,511	11,419	1.31	14,959
1981	448,517	436,407	12,110	1.40	16,954
1982	475,652	462,809	12,843	1.50	19,265
1983	504,429	490,809	13,620	1.61	21,928
1984	534,947	520,503	14,444	1.72	24,844
1985	567,311	551,994	15,317	1.84	28,183
1986	601,633	585,389	16,244	1.97	32,001
1987	638,032	620,805	17,227	2.10	36,177
1988	676,633	658,364	18,269	2.25	41,105
1989	717,569	698,195	19,374	2.41	46,691
1990	760,982	740,435	20,547	2.58	53,011
1991	807,021	785,231	21,790	2.76	60,140
1992	855,846	832,738	23,108	2.95	68,169
1993	907,625	883,119	24,506	3.16	77,439
1994	962,536	936,548	25,988	3.38	87,839

Table 4-40

New Debt Estimates for Northwest Airlines with 1976 Operating Ratio of .893

(thousands of dollars)

Year	Operating Revenues (1976 Dollars)	Operating Expenses (1976 Dollars)	Operating Earnings (1976 Dollars)	Inflation Factor (7 Percent)	Operating Earnings (Current Dollars)
1977-1979	3,255,609	2,907,259	348,350	1.14	397,119
1980	1,219,082	1,088,640	130,442	1.31	170,879
1981	1,292,836	1,154,503	138,333	1.40	193,666
1982	1,371,053	1,224,350	146,703	1.50	220,055
1983	1,454,002	1,298,424	155,578	1.61	250,481
1984	1,541,969	1,376,978	164,991	1.72	283,785
1985	1,635,258	1,460,285	174,973	1.84	321,950
1986	1,734,191	1,548,633	185,558	1.97	365,549
1987	1,839,110	1,642,325	196,785	2.10	413,249
1988	1,950,376	1,741,686	208,690	2.25	469,553
1989	2,068,374	1,847,058	221,316	2.41	533,372
1990	2,193,511	1,958,005	234,706	2.58	605,541
1991	2,326,218	2,077,313	248,905	2.76	686,978
1992	2,466,954	2,202,990	263,964	2.95	778,694
1993	2,616,205	2,336,271	279,934	3.16	884,591
1994	2,774,485	2,477,615	296,870	3.38	1,003,421

Table 4-41

New Debt Estimates for Pan American with 1976 Operating Ratio of .989

(thousands of dollars)

Year	Operating Revenues (1976 Dollars)	Operating Expenses (1976 Dollars)	Operating Earnings (1976 Dollars)	Inflation Factor (7 Percent)	Operating Earnings (Current Dollars)
1977-1979	5,613,333	5,551,586	61,747	1.14	70,392
1980	2,101,946	2,078,825	23,121	1.31	30,289
1981	2,229,114	2,204,594	24,520	1.40	34,328
1982	2,363,975	2,337,971	26,004	1.50	39,006
1983	2,506,995	2,479,418	27,577	1.61	44,399
1984	2,658,668	2,629,423	29,245	1.72	50,301
1985	2,819,517	2,788,502	31,015	1.84	57,068
1986	2,990,098	2,957,207	32,891	1.97	64,795
1987	3,170,999	3,136,118	34,881	2.10	73,250
1988	3,362,844	3,325,853	36,991	2.25	83,230
1989	3,566,296	3,527,067	39,229	2.41	94,542
1990	3,782,057	3,740,454	41,603	2.58	107,336
1991	4,010,871	3,966,751	44,120	2.76	121,771
1992	4,253,529	4,206,740	46,789	2.95	138,028
1993	4,510,868	4,461,248	49,620	3.16	156,799
1994	4,783,776	4,731,154	52,622	3.38	177,862

Table 4-42
New Debt Estimates for Trans World Airlines with 1976 Operating Ratio of .973
(thousands of dollars)

Year	Operating Revenues (1976 Dollars)	Operating Expenses (1976 Dollars)	Operating Earnings (1976 Dollars)	Inflation Factor (7 Percent)	Operating Earnings (Current Dollars)
1977-					
1979	7,035,748	6,845,783	189,965	1.14	216,560
1980	2,634,578	2,563,444	71,134	1.31	93,186
1981	2,793,970	2,718,533	75,437	1.40	105,612
1982	2,963,005	2,883,004	80,001	1.50	120,002
1983	3,142,267	3,057,426	84,841	1.61	136,594
1984	3,332,374	3,242,400	89,974	1.72	154,755
1985	3,533,983	3,438,565	95,418	1.84	175,569
1986	3,747,789	3,646,599	101,190	1.97	199,344
1987	3,974,530	3,867,218	107,312	2.10	225,355
1988	4,214,989	4,101,184	113,805	2.25	256,061
1989	4,469,996	4,349,306	120,690	2.41	290,863
1990	4,740,431	4,612,439	127,992	2.58	330,219
1991	5,027,227	4,891,492	135,735	2.76	374,629
1992	5,331,374	5,187,427	143,947	2.95	424,644
1993	5,653,922	5,501,266	152,656	3.16	482,393
1994	5,995,984	5,834,092	161,892	3.38	547,195

Table 4-43
New Debt Estimates for United Airlines with 1976 Operating Ratio of .986
(thousands of dollars)

Year	Operating Revenues (1976 Dollars)	Operating Expenses (1976 Dollars)	Operating Earnings (1976 Dollars)	Inflation Factor (7 Percent)	Operating Earnings (Current Dollars)
1977-					
1979	8,733,133	8,610,869	122,264	1.14	139,381
1980	3,270,174	3,224,392	45,782	1.31	59,974
1981	3,468,020	3,419,468	48,552	1.40	67,973
1982	3,677,835	3,626,345	51,490	1.50	77,235
1983	3,900,344	3,845,739	54,605	1.61	87,914
1984	4,136,315	4,078,407	57,908	1.72	99,602
1985	4,386,562	4,325,150	61,412	1.84	112,998
1986	4,651,949	4,586,822	65,127	1.97	128,300
1987	4,933,392	4,864,325	69,067	2.10	145,041
1988	5,231,862	5,158,616	73,246	2.25	164,804
1989	5,548,390	5,470,713	77,677	2.41	187,202
1990	5,884,068	5,801,691	82,377	2.58	212,533
1991	6,240,054	6,152,693	87,361	2.76	241,116
1992	6,617,577	6,524,931	92,646	2.95	273,306
1993	7,017,940	6,919,689	98,251	3.16	310,473
1994	7,442,525	7,338,330	104,195	3.38	352,179

Table 4-44

New Debt Estimates for Western Airlines with 1976 Operating Ratio of .951

(thousands of dollars)

Year	Operating Revenues (1976 Dollars)	Operating Expenses (1976 Dollars)	Operating Earnings (1976 Dollars)	Inflation Factor (7 Percent)	Operating Earnings (Current Dollars)
1977-					
1979	2,044,299	1,944,128	100,171	1.14	114,195
1980	765,500	727,991	37,509	1.31	49,137
1981	811,813	772,034	39,779	1.40	55,691
1982	860,928	818,743	42,185	1.50	63,278
1983	913,014	868,276	44,738	1.61	72,028
1984	968,251	920,807	47,444	1.72	81,604
1985	1,026,830	976,515	50,315	1.84	92,580
1986	1,088,953	1,035,594	53,359	1.97	105,117
1987	1,154,835	1,098,248	56,587	2.10	118,833
1988	1,224,703	1,164,693	60,010	2.25	135,023
1989	1,298,798	1,235,157	63,641	2.41	153,375
1990	1,377,375	1,309,884	67,491	2.58	174,127
1991	1,460,706	1,389,131	71,575	2.76	197,547
1992	1,549,079	1,473,174	75,905	2.95	223,920
1993	1,642,798	1,562,301	80,497	3.16	254,371
1994	1,742,187	1,656,820	85,367	3.38	288,540

1976 as opposed to 37,087 on December 31, 1976, a 3 percent drop).[7] Fuel expense rose by a more dramatic percentage (167.9 percent),[8] but actually less in dollar terms than wages and benefits ($208.3 million for fuel—from $124.1 million in 1969 to $332.3 million in 1976).[9] This represents an annual compound rate of wage increase of approximately 10 percent. During this same seven-year period revenue yield per passenger mile rose only 36.8 percent, from $.0562 in 1969 to $.0579 in 1976.

Braniff International Corporation

If Braniff succeeds in maintaining the operating ratio it enjoyed for the five years ended December 31, 1976, it will have a surplus investment potential of $984.8 million by the end of 1985 and $2.3 billion by the end of 1989. If the Company sustains its 1976 operating ratio (.922) for the period in question, the surplus will be $701.4 million by December 31, 1985 and $1.8 billion by the end of 1989. Braniff accomplished this with a load factor far lower than American's—51.9 percent as opposed to American's 58.9 percent. The principal reason for the disparity does not concern expense control. On the contrary, operating expenses per revenue passenger mile were lower for American and only

Table 4-45
Shortage and Surplus Estimates for American Airlines
(thousands of dollars)

Year	Equity	Capital Availability Revised for Interest on New Debt (Cumulative)
	Best Case	
1977-		
1979	735,379	(440,917.5)
1980	814,189	(404,632.0)
1981	910,054	(394,772.5)
1982	1,025,710	(664,955.5)
1983	1,164,259	(1,018,212.5)
1984	1,327,506	(1,456,336.0)
1985	1,519,017	(2,385,420.5)
1986	1,724,386	(3,525,917.0)
1987	2,000,486	(4,354,243.0)
1988	2,299,133	(5,769,003.0)
1989	2,643,808	(6,326,139.0)
	Worst Case	
1977-		
1979	536,174	(631,122.5)
1980	533,140	(873,205.0)
1981	536,247	(1,142,758.5)
1982	546,507	(1,622,141.5)
1983	565,087	(2,178,350.5)
1984	592,413	(2,838,264.0)
1985	629,723	(3,558,070.0)
1986	678,008	(5,030,351.5)
1987	738,179	(6,547,839.5)
1988	811,927	(7,623,192.5)
1989	901,139	(7,432,781.0)

Note: Parentheses indicate shortfalls.

slightly higher than Braniff's for TWA. The difference lies in price per mile charged (see table 4-56).

Braniff's yield (revenue per passenger mile) was $.084 as opposed to $.076 for American and $.075 for TWA. Had American realized this yield, its operating ratio would have been significantly better than the .939 needed to achieve capital self-sufficiency.

If Braniff can continue to generate the earnings it has, the company should not encounter problems relative to capital needs in the 1980s. Helping Braniff is the relatively low degree of competition on its route structure. Braniff flies 33.6 percent of its domestic traffic in monopoly markets. This compares with other carriers as follows:[11] Western—33 percent; United—31.9 percent; Delta—28.8 percent; Eastern—26 percent; and Northwest—23.6 percent.

Table 4-46
Shortage and Surplus Estimates for Braniff International Corporation
(thousands of dollars)

Year	Equity	Capital Availability Revised for Interest on New Debt (Cumulative)
		Best Case
1977-		
1979	282,767	121,248.5
1980	343,015	295,284.5
1981	423,794	481,291.5
1982	521,839	678,327.5
1983	639,776	913,093.0
1984	781,102	1,093,653.5
1985	948,816	984,783.0
1986	1,142,759	1,341,702.0
1987	1,373,231	1,643,936.5
1988	1,635,929	1,995,937.0
1989	1,935,130	2,345,679.5
		Worst Case
1977-		
1979	259,388	66,957.5
1980	309,577	215,296.5
1981	378,954	371,481.5
1982	464,043	533,947.5
1983	567,234	728,690.0
1984	691,853	863,229.0
1985	840,613	701,420.5
1986	1,013,036	997,545.5
1987	1,219,179	1,230,311.0
1988	1,454,233	1,502,709.5
1989	1,746,132	1,817,294.5

Note: Parentheses indicate shortfalls.

Continental Airlines

The estimates for Continental likewise indicate a strong financial posture.

Excess financing potential through December 31, 1985:

Best case	$610.3 million
Worst case	$154.0 million

Excess financing potential through December 31, 1989:

Best case	$1,265.9 million
Worst case	$250.7 million

Table 4-47
Shortage and Surplus Estimates for Continental Airlines
(thousands of dollars)

Year	Equity	Capital Availability Revised for Interest on New Debt (Cumulative)
		Best Case
1977-		
1979	62,068	(71,474.0)
1980	85,705	(184,029.5)
1981	121,092	(99,941.5)
1982	179,066	30,417.5
1983	251,229	179,324.5
1984	347,688	370,915.0
1985	466,658	610,342.0
1986	603,588	543,571.5
1987	760,146	760,008.5
1988	951,082	928,398.5
1989	1,158,699	1,265,919.5
		Worst Case
1977-		
1979	22,527	(81,015.0)
1980	29,149	(210,585.5)
1981	45,253	(196,803.5)
1982	81,316	(162,189.5)
1983	128,539	(85,303.5)
1984	196,742	16,870.0
1985	283,101	154,001.0
1986	383,633	(12,695.5)
1987	499,023	75,870.5
1988	634,171	78,416.5
1989	788,681	250,708.5

Note: Parentheses indicate shortfalls.

Table 4-48
Shortage and Surplus Estimates for Delta Airlines
(thousands of dollars)

Year	Equity (Best Case)	Equity (Worst Case)
1977-		
1979	764,857	711,869
1980	916,922	841,133
1981	1,157,891	1,056,261
1982	1,434,665	1,303,673
1983	1,750,557	1,586,141
1984	2,109,236	1,906,954
1985	2,517,413	2,273,173
1986	2,982,334	2,688,317
1987	3,509,230	3,160,074
1988	4,107,917	3,696,107
1989	4,787,973	4,304,996

Table 4-49
Shortage and Surplus Estimates for Eastern Airlines
(thousands of dollars)

Year	Equity	Capital Availability Revised for Interest on New Debt (Cumulative)
		Best Case
1977-		
1979	250,831	(338,281.0)
1980	269,299	(469,573.5)
1981	359,698	(530,793.5)
1982	473,711	(653,928.5)
1983	620,971	(752,374.0)
1984	804,835	(843,314.5)
1985	1,020,900	(1,086,149.5)
1986	1,271,846	(2,004,821.5)
1987	1,574,017	(2,210,026.5)
1988	1,920,917	(2,143,306.5)
1989	2,318,094	(1,980,716.0)
		Worst Case
1977-		
1979	117,271	(471,841.0)
1980	78,268	(655,604.5)
1981	103,534	(835,130.5)
1982	143,537	(1,246,510.5)
1983	206,555	(1,610,516.0)
1984	294,976	(1,829,521.0)
1985	401,932	(2,194,796.0)
1986	529,937	(3,372,101.0)
1987	693,123	(3,778,498.0)
1988	882,102	(3,935,746.0)
1989	1,099,895	(4,348,077.5)

Note: Parentheses indicate shortfalls.

The success of Continental and an analysis thereof enables one to dispel several myths about the industry and its operating characteristics. One is that the cost structure of the airlines could be radically altered by reducing amenities or the "frills" accorded to passengers. Continental, an extremely successful carrier, does not attempt to conceal that its goal is to provide maximum service to its customers: "Your airline continued to offer extras to the traveling public by way of innovative marketing techniques which brought zest ... to cabin services."[12]

Why, one may ask, were such amenities foregone by various carriers offering dramatically lower fares for so-called "no frills" travel? The answer lies in the regulated structure of the industry. For one airline to offer a lower price for travel between given points than another carrier, the service must be differentiated in terms acceptable to the CAB. The introduction of no frills service was an attempt to gauge the price elasticity of demand, and an experiment in market segmentation in order to compete more effectively for travelers.

Table 4-50
Shortage and Surplus Estimates for National Airlines
(thousands of dollars)

Year	Equity	Capital Availability Revised for Interest on New Debt (Cumulative)
	Best Case	
1977-		
1979	238,714	276,645.5
1980	272,121	361,197.5
1981	315,560	442,257.0
1982	369,582	471,831.0
1983	450,795	470,155.0
1984	542,806	386,439.5
1985	647,191	464,741.5
1986	765,712	25,609.5
1987	899,698	184,532.5
1988	1,051,940	369,204.5
1989	1,224,874	366,595.5
	Worst Case	
1977-		
1979	144,721	(58,372.5)
1980	137,683	(77,142.5)
1981	135,103	(115,925.0)
1982	137,042	(216,323.0)
1983	158,970	(357,235.0)
1984	183,814	(431,414.5)
1985	211,997	(531,050.5)
1986	243,998	(1,123,294.5)
1987	280,175	(1,152,351.5)
1988	321,280	(1,195,777.5)
1989	367,971	(1,451,416.5)

Note: Parentheses indicate shortfalls.

Another fact one is able to uncover is that Continental's actual capital structure is no more leveraged than most of the carriers in this study. Allusion has been made to the relatively heavy debt burden this company must carry. A brokerage study of the industry speaks of the "current weakness of the company's balance sheet."[13] When we take into consideration capital leases—of which the company has none—Continental's capital structure appears reasonable.

The company's expense per revenue passenger mile of $.0805 is low relative to other carriers, giving one a clue to the airline's success. American's 1976 expense per revenue passenger mile was $.0839. Delta's expense per available passenger mile was $.045, as opposed to American's $.049. Northwest's is only $.080 per revenue passenger mile and an incredibly low $.0387 per available passenger mile. The reason for the wide difference between Northwest's cost per available passenger mile and cost per revenue passenger mile relative to that of the other carriers is that Northwest had the lowest passenger load factor in 1976—48.4 percent.

It is now possible to ask several pivotal questions, the answers to which shed

Table 4-51
Surplus and Shortage Estimates for Northwest Airlines
(thousands of dollars)

Year	Equity	Capital Availability Revised for Interest on New Debt (Cumulative)
		Best Case
1977-		
1979	958,389	1,446,725.0
1980	1,108,812	1,813,935.0
1981	1,283,986	2,209,176.0
1982	1,486,393	2,618,759.5
1983	1,736,874	2,965,648.5
1984	2,020,659	3,372,251.0
1985	2,342,609	3,883,786.0
1986	2,708,158	4,027,100.0
1987	3,121,407	4,341,059.5
1988	3,590,960	4,246,874.0
1989	4,124,332	4,665,416.5
		Worst Case
1977-		
1979	876,739	1,257,116
1980	992,028	1,534,571.5
1981	1,127,383	1,825,666.5
1982	1,284,545	2,114,519.0
1983	1,483,525	2,341,637.0
1984	1,708,960	2,567,403.5
1985	1,964,714	2,894,046.5
1986	2,255,104	2,825,034.5
1987	2,583,384	2,906,371.0
1988	2,956,394	2,544,188.5
1989	3,380,101	2,654,609.0

light on the most important issues impacting differentials in financial performance among airlines. The first question is this: Why is there a significant cost differential per available seat mile between, for example, Braniff or Delta and American? Part of the answer lies in such factors as relative fleet age, length of average haul, and efficiency in controlling overhead costs. To a large extent, however, the answer lies in cost differentials for fuel and landing fees in different geographic locales. The following example typifies the problem:[14]

	Dallas/Fort Worth to New York City	San Francisco to Oklahoma City
Mileage	1,384	1,383
Fuel Cost	$59.95	$53.65
Landing Fee	4.86	1.63
Terminal Expense	2.52	4.08
Total Expense	$67.33	$59.36

Table 4-52
Shortage and Surplus Estimates for Pan American World Airways
(thousands of dollars)

Year	Equity (Best Case)
1977-79	126,014
1980	66,191
1981	14,001
1982	(29,913)
1983	(64,840)
1984	(90,267)
1985	(105,291)
1986	(108,034)
1987	(95,238)
1988	(68,341)
1989	(24,203)

Note: The data suggest that there will be a deficit in stockholders' equity even if the "best case" scenario is achieved. No debt issuance would be possible; hence the unadjusted estimate is final. The "worst case" equity deficit is not presented, since even the above performance implies bankruptcy. The company must improve on the performance of recent years in order to survive.
Parentheses indicate shortfalls.

The CAB fare formula is based on average industry costs. The present fare structure generates a subsidy to certain areas and carriers paid by others. The result is "that carriers operating in high-cost areas are discriminated against, while carriers operating in low-cost areas, such as Delta and Braniff, receive a revenue windfall."[15]

While American is impacted by this, TWA, Pan American, and Eastern are also affected, in many cases even more so. Fuel is not the only expense that is higher in the Northeast:

The domestic average weighted landing fee for the ten domestic trunk carriers in 1976 was 55 cents per 1,000 pounds landed, or 13 cents lower than American Airlines' domestic average rate of 68 cents. Under current rate-making philosophy, this difference represents an unrecovered cost to American Airlines. ... [W]e landed 17% of our total system weight in 1976 at high-cost New York City airports, compared with 6% for United. If (American) paid United's average landing fee ... [American's] annual landing fee expense would be reduced— and profits improved—by $7.3 million.[16]

Since New York has been a traditional hub for international traffic—and therefore for Pan American and TWA—these carriers have likewise been affected by high costs of an uncontrollable nature.

Regulatory distortions, therefore, emerge as a key explanatory variable of differentials in profitability among the several carriers, and, one step removed, in their ability to finance needed investment.

Table 4-53
Shortage and Surplus Estimates for Trans World Airlines
(thousands of dollars)

Year	Equity	Capital Availability Revised for Interest on New Debt (Cumulative)
		Best Case
1977-		
1979	59,217	(629,090.5)
1980	24,663	(1,019,859.5)
1981	25,581	(1,167,056.5)
1982	72,874	(1,517,313.5)
1983	146,642	(1,838,873.5)
1984	247,304	(2,538,460.0)
1985	373,015	(2,963,473.0)
1986	541,609	(3,419,380.5)
1987	737,508	(4,066,566.0)
1988	966,054	(4,864,850.0)
1989	1,230,697	(5,228,776.5)
		Worst Case
1977-		
1979	(53,075)	(629,090.5)
1980	(135,949)	(1,068,179.5)
1981	(186,794)	(1,270,139.5)
1982	(201,726)	(1,682,621.5)
1983	(208,787)	(2,085,010.5)
1984	(188,370)	(2,864,842.0)
1985	(153,697)	(3,600,417.0)
1986	(88,469)	(4,398,594.5)
1987	(9,422)	(5,343,413.0)
1988	95,347	(6,426,310.0)
1989	209,167	(7,021,586.5)

Note: Parentheses indicate shortfalls.

Delta Airlines

Turning to Delta Airlines, our findings are as follows:

Excess financing potential through December 31, 1985:

Best case	$3.5 billion
Worst case	$3.0 billion

Excess financing potential through December 31, 1989:

Best case	$5.0 billion
Worst case	$4.0 billion

Delta's 1976 performance was remarkable by any standard. While American's operating income was $71.8 million (on assets of $1.7 billion), Delta's operating income was $117.6 million (on $1.5 billion in assets). American can

Table 4-54
Shortage Surplus and Estimates for United Airlines
(thousands of dollars)

Year	Equity	Capital Availability Revised for Interest on New Debt (Cumulative)
	Best Case	
1977-		
1979	533,605	(577,685.0)
1980	532,238	(729,443.0)
1981	549,474	(952,698.0)
1982	587,205	(1,358,398.0)
1983	648,314	(1,777,437.0)
1984	739,929	(2,501,438.0)
1985	857,868	(3,394,748.0)
1986	1,021,002	(5,338,320.0)
1987	1,213,743	(6,598,336.0)
1988	1,440,835	(7,232,256.0)
1989	1,709,112	(7,694,895.0)
	Worst Case	
1977-		
1979	453,959	(657,331.0)
1980	428,319	(843,362.0)
1981	406,714	(1,105,458.0)
1982	400,312	(1,671,514.0)
1983	411,184	(2,273,608.0)
1984	445,883	(3,088,069.0)
1985	499,253	(4,081,124.0)
1986	589,071	(6,134,829.0)
1987	698,929	(7,516,208.0)
1988	831,848	(8,284,970.0)
1989	993,150	(8,897,824.0)

Note: Parentheses indicate shortfalls.

not explain away Delta's performance simply by indicating that Delta serves lower cost areas, at least in 1976. At that time American enjoyed the benefits of an extremely favorable fuel contract entered into in 1974. American's cost per gallon was 27.5 cents as opposed to 30.0 cents for Delta. Had American paid for fuel at Delta's rate, operating income would have been reduced by about $30 million. American did have higher landing fees, $55.4 million or .24 cents per revenue passenger mile as opposed to $31.8 million or .18 cents per revenue passenger mile for Delta.[17] General and administrative expense for American totaled $91.3 million or .396 cents per revenue passenger mile, whereas Delta's general and administrative expense was $47.1 million or .268 cents per revenue passenger mile. Even had Delta incurred American's ratio of general and administrative expense to revenue passenger miles, total operating expense per revenue passenger mile would still be 8.14 cents as opposed to 8.39 cents for American. This indicates that nondiscretionary costs such as differentials in

Table 4-55
Shortage and Surplus Estimates for Western Airlines
(thousands of dollars)

Year	Equity	Capital Availability Revised for Interest on New Debt (Cumulative)
		Best Case
1977-		
1979	176,497	51,337.5
1980	212,401	88,627.0
1981	257,320	131,818.0
1982	315,189	227,263.5
1983	388,438	269,643.5
1984	473,698	290,368.5
1985	578,965	327,068.5
1986	700,876	76,117.0
1987	839,118	(111,593.0)
1988	996,720	92,369.0
1989	1,176,139	324,987.5
		Worst Case
1977-		
1979	155,523	2,631.5
1980	182,401	16,864.0
1981	217,092	33,303.0
1982	263,338	97,734.5
1983	323,357	104,205.5
1984	393,628	124,795.5
1985	481,892	114,333.5
1986	584,497	(187,164.0)
1987	700,914	(428,048.0)
1988	833,715	(294,300.0)
1989	984,964	(142,199.5)

Note: Parentheses indicate shortfalls.

landing fees and terminal expense probably account for the remainder of the difference. We can state this since the only other largely discretionary area—promotion and sales—was almost identical (.969 cents and .995 cents per revenue passenger mile for Delta and American, respectively). Had Delta incurred promotional expenses equal to American's, its total operating expenses would have risen from our restated 8.14 cents to 8.16 cents per revenue passenger mile. American's 8.39 cents operating expense per revenue passenger mile would still be 2.8 percent higher holding the above discretionary costs constant.

This comparison has been carried to significant lengths since these carriers represent crucial aspects of the fundamental questions being asked. Delta is a successful airline that will probably not experience any financing difficulties whatever. American, like United, is a successful though less profitable airline that will probably encounter severe problems in meeting its capital expenditure

Table 4-56
Comparative Unit Revenue and Expense for Three Airlines (1976)

Category	American	Braniff	Trans World
Operating Expense	$1,936,124	$622,112	$2,024,000
Revenue passenger miles (thousands)	23,072,000	6,911,942	22,295,300
Expense per revenue passenger mile	$.08392	$.0900	$.09078
Yield	$.076	$.084	$.075

requirements in the years ahead. The difference between American and Delta with respect to operating expenses is 2.8 percent. Discretionary costs and relative fleet efficiencies (fuel usage per revenue passenger mile) have been held constant, and it appears that the difference can be explained only in terms of regulatory policy.

Eastern Airlines

Eastern Airlines is a unique and troubled corporation attempting to stage a comeback from the brink of insolvency. The findings of this study with respect to Eastern's ability to raise needed capital are as follows:

Shortfall in financing through December 31, 1985:

Best case	$1,086.1 million
Worst case	$2,194.8 million

Shortfall in financing through December 31, 1989:

Best case	$1,980.7 million
Worst case	$4,348.1 million

Eastern's 1976 operating expense was an extremely high 8.95 cents per revenue passenger mile. Its operating expense per available seat mile was 5.03 cents compared with 4.64 cents for Delta and 4.91 cents for American.

The *Wall Street Journal* indicated that "Eastern, already loaded with debt, doesn't have any money to buy new planes."[18] On December 31, 1976 Eastern's debt-to-equity ratio, including capital leases, was a crushing 82/18. The uncertainties surrounding the purchase of the A300 Airbus have been resolved.[19] To gain access to the once impenetrable American market, the European consortium has agreed to sell Eastern twenty-five of the aircraft, and to guarantee the carrier's borrowings in conjunction with the sale. The present study estimates that the 5,725 seats so acquired will only accommodate

Eastern's needs until sometime in 1982. When one looks beyond the aggregate capacity requirements to qualitative factors, the picture is even less favorable:

> The major waster of money is Eastern's fleet. The airline has far too many little planes. . . . Because of such inefficiencies, Eastern's costs for each ton of freight and passengers flown one mile were 40¢ in 1976, the highest in the industry.[20]

It was noted previously that Eastern's 1976 operating expense was 8.95 cents per revenue passenger mile and 5.03 cents per available seat mile. The corresponding amounts for TWA are 5.15 cents and 9.08 cents, respectively. This higher amount for TWA is attributable to the much higher cost of fuel abroad. Among the domestic carriers, Eastern's 1976 cost structure was the highest.

The Airbus purchase will hardly be a panacea for Eastern's deep-rooted problems:

> U.S. airlines haven't ordered European jets in over 15 years; those they did order quickly proved inefficient on U.S. routes. Even if the new Airbus turned out to be a good plane, some airline executives worry that Eastern, already saddled with a huge debt, would be risking too much by taking on more debt to acquire the new craft.[21]

American required only 90 percent as many employees per available passenger seat mile as Eastern in 1975. Eastern's fuel expense per available seat mile was 18.6 percent higher than American's, due both to a higher cost paid per gallon and to Eastern's less efficient fleet. The two great conditions for Eastern's survival are (1) continued profitability in the short run to offset a crushing debt repayment schedule; and (2) eventual fleet rationalization to make Eastern a more viable competitor with respect to cost.

Eastern will have to maintain the "best case" operating ratio of .956 to survive the coming years. A return to the five-year average operating ratio of .975 would bring the corporation to the brink of default by 1981 and eliminate its ability to raise the capital needed to attempt a comeback. Should this scenario unfold, it is highly likely that Delta and National would expand to fill the void, effectively reducing Eastern's market share and worsening the company's relative competitive position.

National Airlines

National Airlines is a relatively small though successful carrier. The findings with respect to the Company's ability to finance its forthcoming capital needs are as follows:

> Excess (deficit) in financing potential through December 31, 1985:
> Best case $464.7 million
> Worst case $531.1 million

Excess (deficit) in financing potential through December 31, 1989:

Best case $366.6 million
Worst case $1,451.4 million

National is fortunate, since "the Company's present fleet is modern and one of the most efficient in the industry."[22]

One of National's prime objectives has been fleet standardization. The company sold its Boeing 747's, and now has only 727's and DC-10's. National's operating expenses were 4.23 cents per available seat mile in 1976, as opposed to 4.72 cents for American and 4.99 cents for Eastern. In addition to economies stemming from a relatively efficient fleet, National also enjoys the favorable geographic cost effects that have aided Braniff and Delta.

Northwest Airlines

The analysis of Northwest's ability to finance its capital needs yields the following:

Excess financing potential for the period ending December 31, 1989:
Best case $4,665.4 million
Worst case $2,654.6 million

Excess financing potential for the period ending December 31, 1985:
Best case $3,883.8 million
Worst case $2,894.0 million

Northwest's 1976 operating expense per available seat mile was an incredibly low 3.88 cents. Operating expense per revenue passenger mile is somewhat closer to that of the other carriers, since Northwest's load factor is substantially lower. For Northwest, the cost is 8.0 cents, compared with 8.40 cents for American— still a significantly lower amount. The success, however, has not been achieved without another cost. The company has been plagued with labor confrontations: "Since 1960, there have been eight strikes at Northwest, totaling more than 550 days."[23] At the end of June 1978, a strike which began April 30 was still in progress. A key issue was the pilots' demand for increased rest time during long flights. "The Company has opposed the idea as featherbedding, while the pilots insist it is important to passenger safety."[24]

Wall Street is not as yet alarmed by Northwest's difficulties. The *New York Times* quoted Julius Maldutis, vice-president of the transportation group at Salomon Brothers as saying: "Northwest is consistently profitable and gets more productivity from fewer people than any airline in the industry."[25]

One factor enabling Northwest to endure the financial impact of long strikes is a so-called "mutual aid agreement" among airlines, whereby nonstruck member carriers guarantee to pay a certain percentage of a struck member carrier's expenses, and to reimburse the struck carrier for the windfall gains accruing to them during the strike. While it appears that Northwest is in the strongest position of any airline, that generally held belief must be qualified with respect to labor uncertainties.

Pan American World Airways

The present study indicates the following with respect to Pan American's ability to raise needed capital:

Shortfall in financing through December 31, 1985:
Best case $2.80 billion
Worst case $3.71 billion

Shortfall in financing through December 31, 1989:
Best case $7.01 billion
Worst case $9.64 billion

The "best case" earnings assumption for this study of .989 experienced in 1976 is not enough to prevent bankruptcy in the years ahead. Even this earnings assumption leaves a deficit in stockholders' equity during the period 1982 through 1989. Survival necessitates a sharp improvement in earnings.

In 1976 Pan American purchased 49 percent of its fuel abroad. Cost per gallon in December 1976 averaged 39.12 cents, significantly higher than the domestic price.[26] Pan American's debt-to-equity ratio on December 31, 1976 was 79/21, taking into account capital leases. As indicated earlier, "Pan Am's Loan and Credit agreements generally prohibit Pan Am from acquiring, leasing, or creating security interests in additional aircraft."[27] The extraordinarily high December 31, 1976 debt-to-equity ratio actually reflects an improvement from earlier in the year, since in April the company experienced a $117.5 million gain on exchanging convertible debentures for ones with later maturities and a lower exercise price.

In 1975 Pan American's operating expense per available seat mile was 5.19 cents, and expense per revenue passenger mile was 10.95 cents. In 1975 Pan American incurred fuel expense of $349.4 million in flying 31.38 million available seat miles. Had Pan American purchased fuel at American's rate (26.5 cents per gallon) instead of its own rate (37.14 cents per gallon), its total operating expense would have been approximately $100 million less.

For the eight years ended December 31, 1976, Pan American suffered a net loss before extraordinary items of $323.2 million. In no year was the company profitable. It is competing against state-owned foreign carriers who are often willing to incur a loss in order to encourage tourism and foster the receipt of foreign exchange. In addition to this problem, "the average age of Pan Am's fleet is among the highest in the industry."[28] As with Eastern and TWA, the company's long-term survival is in serious jeopardy.

Trans World Airlines

TWA's debt-to-equity ratio on December 31, 1976, including capital leases, was 81/19. TWA's ratio of fuel consumed to available seat miles flown is 1.44 percent higher than American's. Since American has a relatively old fleet, TWA's fleet is among the least efficient in the industry. The findings with respect to Trans World's ability to raise needed capital in the years ahead are as follows:

> Shortfall in financing through December 31, 1985:
> Best case $2.96 billion
> Worst case $3.60 billion
>
> Shortfall through December 31, 1989:
> Best case $5.23 billion
> Worst case $7.02 billion

TWA's management is aware of the problems that lie ahead. In his 1976 letter to stockholders, the airline's president indicated the following:

> One of the principal challenges I face as President of TWA is the prospective need to modify and/or replace large numbers of aircraft. Much of TWA's fleet is growing old and will require replacement . . . during the 1980's. . . . If we are unsuccessful, the result can only be a net reduction in the size of the airline.[29]

For TWA to finance its capital needs, this study estimates that its operating ratio must remain no higher than 94.2 percent—significantly better than the "best case" 1976 operating ratio of .973. In recent times the company has demonstrated considerable improvement. It must, however, overcome its huge debt burden in time to finance forthcoming capital needs.

An article appearing in *Institutional Investor* analyzed the magnitude of the Corporation's problems:

> The stark reality is that TWA, in order to stay in the running, must somehow raise $3 billion of fresh capital between now and 1985. The alternative, if not extinction, is a drastic contraction of its present operations. The men who run and finance TWA think they can pull it off. But analysts and bankers, viewing the Company's erratic performance of the past ten years, are not so sure.[30]

The article alludes to a $3 billion capital requirement by the end of 1984. The present study estimates $3.8 billion, and an additional $1.1 billion in 1985 alone.

TWA's lack of credibility in the financial community is portrayed as follows:

> Skepticism about TWA's ability to raise $3 billion over the next seven years is not misplaced. This is a company, after all, whose $1.2 billion debt burden is so crushing that it has been prohibited from paying dividends since the second quarter of 1969; a company that in 1976 was so close to violating its loan covenants that it could not repay borrowings under its revolving credit agreement; a company that last year was so desperate for equity that it was willing to consider selling shares at half of book value; and a company that last March had to give senior lenders a mortgage on all its aircraft in order to pay arrearages on its preferred so it could sell more preferred in July.[31]

The article indicates that Wall Street is very dubious regarding TWA's claim that it can achieve and maintain the needed rate of profitability. In acquiring the present generation of aircraft, the 747's and L-1011's in its fleet,

> [the company] announced that improvement of the profit picture by whatever means was essential and for that reason a virtual certainty. Over the next eight years, however, the company was to lose money in three of them and barely break even in one. Nonetheless, by piling on the debt and mortgaging itself to the wingtips, TWA managed to raise $2 billion and by 1976 haul the last of its wide bodied jets in the door. But the result was a staggering 5:1 debt to equity ratio. As a result, TWA faces the 1980's as the most leveraged airline in the industry with an urgent need to raise another $3 billion for the replacement of a good part of its aging, 85 plane, 707 fleet.[32]

An important negative factor to consider is that TWA's subsidiaries—Hilton International and Canteen Corporation—are far more successful than the airline. In September 1977, the Company announced nine-month pretax earnings of $65.9 million:

> What the company is not trumpeting so loudly, however, is that 65% of those earnings came from Hilton International and Canteen Corp. subsidiaries, which together account for only 29% of revenues. As for the airline, which contributes about $2 billion of the company's $2.9 billion revenues, its making even less than it did in 1976—$29.4 million for the first nine months versus $40.9 million last year. The airline is the real problem—especially the domestic airline, a steady loser since 1974.[33]

The article in *Institutional Investor* characterizes TWA as "an airline with costs that are high for its industry and rising, with an international and domestic route structure that is highly seasonal, with a weak balance sheet and a history of uneven profitability.[34]

As a concluding note, the article also cites the issue of possible deregulation "If deregulation means price wars, as many think it will, then the inefficient carriers are the ones that are going to be merged or other wise weeded out."[35] Deregulation may very well not imply price wars, since a generally tight capacity in the industry may render competition for market share pointless.

United Airlines

Two of the three largest transcontinental carriers—American and Trans World—have been scrutinized. The one remaining, the nation's largest airline, is United. The present study estimates United's capital shortfall as follows:

Period ending December 31, 1985:
Best case $3.39 billion
Worst case $4.08 billion

Period ending December 31, 1989:
Best case $7.69 billion
Worst case $8.90 billion

Including the impact of capital leases, United's debt-to-equity ratio was 69/31 on December 31, 1976.

United enjoys the highest load factor in the industry: 59.4 percent in 1976 and 59.9 percent in 1977. A large and successful transcontinental carrier, one must wonder why United—like American—faces an impending capital shortage while another carrier—Delta—does not. Delta's 1976 operating expense per available seat mile was 4.64 cents as opposed to 4.82 cents for United. Delta's yield (revenue per revenue passenger mile) was 8.0 cents as opposed to 7.8 cents for United. Had United enjoyed the yield earned by Delta, the corporation's earnings would have increased $68.4 million. Recall that American's yield was lower than either at 7.60 cents. If Delta had received American's average price, its $109.5 million pretax 1976 earnings would have fallen about $67 million. Had Delta received United's average price per revenue passenger mile, earnings would have dropped about $32 million.

Assuming that United is able to retain the leverage present in its December 31, 1976 financial position, the capital shortage would be reduced as follows:

Shortfall for the period ending December 31, 1985:
Best case $2.53 billion
Worst case $3.58 billion

Shortfall for the period ending December 31, 1989:
Best case $5.98 billion
Worst case $7.90 billion

United recently placed the largest aircraft order in the history of commercial aviation. On July 14, 1978, United "ordered 30 medium-sized, wide body Boeing 767's at a cost of $1.2 billion. . . . [I] t [also] ordered an additional 30 Boeing 727-200's for $400 million."[36] The crucial nature of the decision was well expressed by United's vice-president of operations services, James Hartigan: "It was a deal that could make or break United."[37]

It is generally believed that this order will lend the necessary momentum to Boeing's push to develop the new series of aircraft. "This initial 767 order gave Boeing the thrust it needed to launch a whole family of new wide-body jets, which probably will include a slightly larger trijet, the 777, and a smaller twin-jet, the 757."[38] Both Eastern and British Airways have already indicated their intention to buy the 757. United is expected to acquire options for twelve to fifteen more 767's. United hopes to have the first 767's in service by June 1982 "in about 20 cities, such as Memphis, Raleigh and Fresno, where the traffic hasn't justified jumbo jets but has outgrown the smaller planes."[39]

Among the many advantages of the new plane are the following: (1) The 767 will consume 35 percent less fuel per available seat mile than the DC-8's and 727-100's it will replace; (2) a new wing design will limit turbulence in flight; and (3) it will by quiet aircraft. United has dictated a considerable portion of the specifications for the new aircraft. The initial Boeing design called for one hundred ninety-one seats. United requested two hundred two. A compromise was reached at one hundred ninety-seven seats. As one Boeing executive indicated, "For every four seats you take out of a 200 passenger plane, the cost per seat mile goes up 2%." Airbus had offered United very liberal financing. Boeing's response was, "We finally told United we could build the plane but we couldn't buy it for them."[40] Boeing was able to document greater operating economies and to extend performance guarantees that were superior to Airbus. The guarantees were no small matter to United, "which spent $450 million on maintaining planes last year."[41]

While United faces serious challenges in raising all the capital it will require, the company is strong and respected, and it is unlikely that serious financial difficulties will be encountered.

Western Airlines

Western Airlines, a successful carrier, flew 34 percent as many revenue passenger miles as American in 1976, and 23 percent as many as United. The present study indicates a prospective surplus (shortfall) in financing capabilities as follows:

Period ending December 31, 1985:
Best case $327.1 million
Worst case $114.3 million

Period ending December 31, 1989:
Best case $325.0 million
Worst case   142.2) million   ($142.2) million

The company's debt-to-equity ratio was 66/34 at year end 1976. The company has major reequipment needs, but appears able to maintain a relatively strong balance sheet. As shown in table 4-57,[42] Western's five-year return on equity was a healthy 14.1 percent. The fortunes of the other carriers differ widely, as that table portrays.

It should now be apparent that the industry is hardly homogenous; the fortunes of the corporate entities that comprise it may vary widely in the years ahead. For that reason shortage carriers, ones unable to finance their future capital requirements, will be distinguished from surplus carriers, ones with the financial muscle to expand beyond the scope of their present route structure.

Tables 4-58 and 4-59 indicate the total capital shortfall for the shortage carriers taken separately and the net shortfall if the surplus carriers are allowed to enter markets presently served by the troubled airlines. The term "shortage market" will be used to denote the routes served by carriers for which a capital shortage is indicated.

These tables make the very strong assumption that companies may enter new markets without creating serious dislocations with respect to the operations of carriers already serving those markets. Recent regulatory changes make it possible for companies to enter markets if they can demonstrate that service to a given location will benefit. Cutthroat competition may eventually result, however, and it is conceivable that entry into new markets by strong carriers would force their less successful counterparts out of business.

Table 4-57
Five-Year Average Return on Equity

Company	Percent Return on Equity
American	3.3
Braniff	17.6
Continental	3.5
Delta	17.6
Eastern	Deficit
National	8.9
Northwest	10.1
Pan American	Deficit
Trans World	1.1
United	6.8
Western	14.1

Table 4-58
Capital Availability: Period Ending December 31, 1985
(billions of dollars)

Company	Best Case		Worst Case	
American	(2.4)	(2.4)	(3.6)	(3.6)
Braniff	1.0		0.7	
Continental	0.6		0.2	
Delta	3.5		3.0	
Eastern	(1.1)		(2.2)	(2.2)
National	0.5		(0.5)	(0.5)
Northwest	3.9		2.9	
Pan American	(2.8)	(2.8)	(3.7)	(3.7)
Trans World	(3.0)	(3.0)	(3.6)	(3.6)
United	(3.4)	(3.4)	(4.1)	(4.1)
Western	0.3		0.1	
With entry barrier		(12.7)		(17.7)
Without entry barrier	(2.9)		(10.8)	

Note: Parentheses indicate shortfalls.

It is, therefore, not at all certain that a smooth response to locational shortages through slight increments to service by strong carriers will result when a financially troubled carrier is unable to service a given market adequately. There is a danger that the strong carrier will "invade" the route served by a weaker company and attempt to force the weaker competitor out of the market. If this results, the benefits derived from the entry of the capital-abundant company may be more than offset by the negative impact on the operational viability of the weaker corporation.

Table 4-59
Capital Availability: Period Ending December 31, 1989
(billions of dollars)

Company	Best Case		Worst Case	
American	(6.3)	(6.3)	(7.4)	(7.4)
Braniff	2.3		1.8	
Continental	1.3		0.3	
Delta	5.0		4.0	
Eastern	(2.0)	(2.0)	(4.3)	(4.3)
National	0.4		(1.5)	(1.5)
Northwest	4.7		2.7	
Pan American	(7.0)	(7.0)	(9.6)	(9.6)
Trans World	(5.2)	(5.2)	(7.0)	(7.0)
United	(7.7)	(7.7)	(8.9)	(8.9)
Western	0.3		(0.1)	(0.1)
With barrier to entry		(28.2)		(38.8)
Without entry barrier	(14.2)		(30.0)	

Note: Parentheses indicate shortfalls.

This qualification must be borne in mind when analyzing the following tables, which portray the idealized potential of free entry in reducing the impending capital shortage. The actual dynamics of competition may well vary from these results, which are purely static in nature. The key aspects of tables 4-58 and 4-59 are captured in table 4-60.

A $14.2 billion shortage is the least possible, even assuming (1) no federal income tax; (2) best case operating ratios; and (3) free entry by strong carriers to markets served by financially troubled carriers.

The $14.2 billion appears inevitable, even given these assumptions. Only one further source of private financing can be suggested: additional debt, possibly in the form of leasing. As the CAB has pointed out, "In recent times, leased equipment has more or less stabilized at about 25% of all airline equipment."[43] It would be incorrect to assume, however, that all the carriers would be able to enter into additional leases. Eastern, Pan American, and TWA, for example, would lack the ability to enter into material amounts of new debt in the coming years.

Leases are now capitalized and recorded on the balance sheet. Raising an additional 25 percent of total capital through leasing would raise the debt-to-equity ratios from the 55/45 used in this study to 64/36, raising risk considerably for the industry. Given all the most optimistic occurrences, the industry as a whole could just meet its requirements (table 4-61). Two major facts, however, stand out. One is that the required assumptions are too optimistic. American's retained earnings on December 31, 1976 were actually 3 percent lower than on December 31, 1968. While solvency is certain, cost control has not been adequate, and American's fleet is among the oldest in the industry. The "best case" in this study is not likely to be achieved, and American—unable to pay dividends on its common stock from 1971 until 1978—is going to encounter very serious difficulties in financing its capital needs.

United is the nation's largest carrier and has enormous capital requirements in the years immediately ahead. The company has made substantial purchase commitments to replace its aging fleet, and profit performance has been very erratic in recent years. The "best case" operating ratio is perhaps more realistic than for American, but still higher than that most likely to be attained.

Table 4-60
Summary of Capital Shortage (1976-1989)
(billions of dollars)

Condition	Best Case	Worst Case
With barrier to entry	28.2	38.8
Without barrier to entry	14.2	30.0

Table 4-61
Most Optimistic Surplus (Shortage) by Carrier Through 1989
(billions of dollars)

Carrier	Surplus
American	(3.5)
Braniff	3.0
Continental	1.9
Delta	5.0
Eastern	(2.0)
National	1.1
Northwest	6.4
Pan American	(7.0)
Trans World	(5.2)
United	(3.4)
Western	1.0
Net deficit financing	(2.7)

Note: Parentheses indicate shortfalls.

If the position of American and United can be characterized as difficult, those of Trans World, Pan American and Eastern must be depicted as approaching hopelessness. Even if the "best case" operating ratios can be achieved, the companies will still be reduced in their relative competitive stature. Should they fall far from this most optimistic scenario, bankruptcy is inevitable. A recession anytime from the present through the 1980s will have serious consequences for the industry, and particularly for these marginal survivors.

Delta's position is strong thanks to a modern fleet and effective cost control. "Best case" operating results, however, are not likely to be achieved in the deregulated era. The low cost areas that were its exclusive domain will now be subject to greater competition, and fares should begin to reflect geographic cost differentials. The company is likely to encounter cost pressures which have hurt other carriers as it expands from its current route structure. The same conditions apply to Braniff. Both these carriers, and Northwest, have modern fleets and enjoy the operating economies of newer aircraft. Since fares will be kept identical among the airlines as a competitive necessity, Delta, Braniff, and Northwest—all of whom enjoy cost advantages over United, American, TWA, Pan American, and luckless Eastern—will gain at the expense of these less efficient carriers.

Trans World, Pan American, and Eastern have thus far managed to escape insolvency, but the cost of doing so has been enormous. Mortgaged to the breaking point, they are no longer able to serve fully the market they once did. As needs expand, they will be incapable of meeting them. American and United can expand somewhat, but will have to devote their energies to replacing aging equipment. They will be unable to approach meeting the capacity additions the coming years will call for.

The wide differences in the respective fortunes of the nation's carriers indicates that free entry to alternative markets is essential to tap fully capabilities of the high performance carriers. The major policy implications of these findings include the extension of currently favorable tax legislation and an immediate and comprehensive deregulation of the industry.

The Tax Reform Act of 1976 allowed airlines to offset 100 percent of their taxable income with investment tax credits. The law further allowed airlines to use investment tax credits which had expired during the long years when profits were not to be had.

The most critical policy measure at this juncture is the broadening of income tax liberalization for the airlines in the 1980s. The best approach would be to enlarge the investment tax credit to perhaps 15 percent or 20 percent of the total purchase price of an aircraft. This would facilitate the acquisition of needed capacity and encourage the strong carriers to expand into markets served currently by weak carriers. If tax relief were merely granted through lower tax rates to the airlines as corporations, the windfall might be paid out in dividends or invested in a nonairline subsidiary.

The other key issue is deregulation. A preview of the effects of this trend is reflected in a recent merger development. Continental Airlines and Western Airlines announced that they intend to submit a merger proposal to their boards of directors. The resulting entity would "replace Northwest Airlines as the seventh-largest carrier, with revenues in excess of $1.5 billion."[44] Market forces are said to underlie the move "Analysts cited the long-term effects of deregulation as the reason for renewed interest in airline consolidations."[45] Years of complacency under regulation are giving way to years when survival will emerge as a major objective "The change in regulatory environment means that the strong will get stronger and the weak will get weaker. . . . [T]he smaller lines are trying to strengthen themselves to be in a better position to attract capital."[46]

National Airlines is now being courted by Pan American as well as by a regional carrier, Texas International. A merger with National Airlines would give Pan American crucial "feeder" routes—those beyond the major cities for international flight origination, such as New York. Another extremely important consideration for this merger is its effect on the current problem of seasonality for both carriers. National's business is strongest in the winter; Pan American's in the summer. Fleet consolidation through merger would smooth seasonal peaks and valleys, and higher levels of financial performance would probably result.

Pan American typifies the disastrous impact that overcapacity had in the early 1970s: "This will be Pan Am's second year in the black after an eight year string of losers in which its stockholders' equity dwindled by more than 50% and the company came within a hairsbreadth of bankruptcy."[47] The Company has retrenched by about 25 percent in recent years. An important factor lending stability to the company's operations has been the relative growth in business versus pleasure traffic, from 30 percent in 1970 to 50 percent today. The price of holding on as one observer has noted,

[was] horrendous. In order to raise badly needed capital, Seawell had to issue debentures convertible into common stock, most of them at such a low price that, if they were converted, Pan Am's common capitalization would be 97.9 million shares vs. just 34 million shares as recently as a decade ago.[48]

Western and American attempted to combine in 1973-1974, but the CAB refused to permit the merger. In the early 1960s, American indicated a desire to merge with Eastern, but the Justice Department objected. The logic for either merger is much the same as for a National-Pan American combination. Both Eastern and Western fly primarily north to south along their respective coasts. These routes are most heavily traveled by vacationers going either to warmer climates or to ski areas. American's business is from the East Coast to the West Coast, routes most heavily traveled in the summer months. A combination would reduce this element of seasonality. The same logic led American to acquire Trans Caribbean Airways in 1970 to balance the company's route structure with north-south capabilities.

Deregulation is now a virtual certainty. A bill that calls for the phased implementation of this long-standing goal became law in 1978. Under the terms of this legislation, airlines have been vested with the authority to make marginal adjustments to fares on a discretionary basis. It also fosters competition by expediting the process through which an airline may secure the right to serve a designated location.

The pace of deregulation should have been set more rapidly. The protracted period of doubt will only exacerbate investor uneasiness during a time when capital needs cannot be legislated to remain in abeyance. The law is, nonetheless, a constructive first step.

Notes

1. American Airlines, 1976 *Annual Report*, p. 3.
2. Ibid., p. 22.
3. Ibid., p. 20.
4. American Airlines, 1976 *Annual Report*, p. 22.
5. American Airlines, 1977 *Annual Report*, pp. 34-35.
6. American Airlines, 1976 *Annual Report*, pp. 34-35.
7. Ibid., p. 35.
8. Ibid., p. 20.
9. Ibid., p. 21.
10. Sources for this presentation were the 1976 annual reports for American and Trans World, and *Form 10-K* for Braniff.
11. American Airlines, *Jetlines*, May 26, 1978. Reprinted with permission.
12. Continental Airlines, 1976 *Annual Report*, p. 1.
13. Donaldson, Lufkin, and Jenrette, *Domestic Trunk Airlines: A Shortage Industry In The Making*, section on Continental Airlines.

14. American Airlines, *Jetlines*, May 26, 1978. Reprinted with permission.

15. American Airlines, *Jetlines*, May 26, 1978. Reprinted by permission.

16. Ibid., p. 2.

17. Delta Airlines, 1976 *Form 10-K*, American Airlines *Form S-1.*

18. Reprinted by permission of *The Wall Street Journal* © Dow Jones & Company, Inc. 1978. All rights reserved.

19. *New York Times*, February 17, 1978, p. 1.

20. Reprinted by permission of *The Wall Street Journal* © Dow Jones & Company, Inc. 1978. All rights reserved.

21. Ibid.

22. National Airlines, 1976 *Form 10-K,* p. 13.

23. *New York Times* © by the New York Times Company. Reprinted by permission.

24. Ibid. © by the New York Times Company. Reprinted by permission.

25. Ibid. © by The New York Times Company. Reprinted by permission.

26. Pan American World Airways, 1976 *Form 10-K,* p. 10.

27. Ibid., p. 1.

28. Donaldson, Lufkin, and Jenrette, *Domestic Trunk Airlines*, p. 49.

29. Trans World Airlines, 1976 *Annual Report,* letter from C.E. Meyer, Jr., to stockholders.

30. Julie Connelly, "TWA: A Company in Search of $3 Billion" by Julie Connelly *Institutional Investor,* Dec. 1977 (New York: Institutional Investor Systems), p. 94. Reprinted with permission.

31. Ibid., p. 94. Reprinted with permission.

32. Ibid., p. 95. Reprinted with permission.

33. Ibid., p. 95. Reprinted with permission.

34. Ibid., p. 95. Reprinted with permission.

35. Ibid., p. 95. Reprinted with permission.

36. Byrne and Kelliher, "The Big Buy," the *Wall Street Journal,* September 25, 1978, p. 1. Reprinted with permission.

37. Ibid. Reprinted with permission.

38. Ibid. Reprinted with permission.

39. Ibid., p. 1. Reprinted with permission.

40. Ibid., p. 34. Reprinted with permission.

41. Ibid., p. 34. Reprinted with permission.

42. *Forbes,* January 1978, p. 136.

43. CAB, *Airline Equipment Needs and Financing Through 1985,* D.C.: CAB, 1976), p. 13.

44-46. *New York Times,* © by the New York Times Company. Reprinted by permission.

47. James Cook, "Pan American: Coming Home," *Forbes,* Oct. 16, 1978, p. 47. Reprinted with permission.

48. Ibid., p. 47. Reprinted with permission.

5

Summary

The findings of this study may be summarized as follows.

1. The domestic trunk carriers and Pan American will require $83.8 billion in the period 1977-1989 for the purchase of passenger aircraft.

2. For the airlines to approach meeting this need, measures should be taken by government to grant federal income tax relief, possibly through liberalization of the investment tax credit.

3. The present trend toward deregulation of the industry is deemed to be constructive, and continuation in that direction should be helpful in providing air service where it is most needed.

4. If the airlines in this study could possibly (1) achieve the "best case" operating ratios; (2) maintain a leveraged capital structure (a debt-to-equity ratio of 64/36); (3) obtain federal income tax relief; and if free entry to new routes prevails, then capital requirements might be met. This case is portrayed in table 5-1. A serious qualification to this is that the five deficit carriers shown in table 5-1 are the nation's five largest airlines. This means that the six smaller carriers would have to expand profitably into markets where the larger carriers have experienced acute difficulties.

5. If the competitive capital markets which are anticipated in the years ahead force airlines to adopt more conservative approaches to their respective capital structures, a shortage will materialize. If they can achieve the "best case" operating ratios, and maintain a debt-to-equity ratio of 55/45, an $11.9 billion shortage will develop during the 1980s, even if free entry is allowed and federal income tax relief is obtained. Table 5-2 portrays this scenario. The other is that the fortunes of the carriers involved differ too dramatically to make a judgment for the industry as a whole.

The assumptions necessary to achieve capital sufficiency from an aggregate viewpoint are as follows: (1) "best case" earnings performance in all cases; (2) no federal income tax for any of the carriers over the entire period; (3) free entry to any route by any carrier; (4) ability of the financially successful carriers to maintain "best case" operating ratios without the advantages bestowed upon them in the era of regulation; and (5) the ability to maintain a leveraged posture in highly competitive financial markets.

The wide discrepancy in the financial performance of the several carriers also portends serious problems in the years ahead. Table 4-6 demonstrates that even if the industry shortage were overcome through the highly optimistic

Table 5-1
Capital Needs by Carrier with All Positive Factors Operative
(Debt-to-Equity = 64/36)
(billions of dollars)

Carrier	Capital Requirements	Capital Availability	Percentage Of Requirements Covered
Delta	7.7	14.2	184
Braniff	2.9	5.9	203
Northwest	6.6	13.0	197
Continental	2.3	4.2	183
National	2.9	4.0	138
Western	3.0	4.0	133
Eastern	9.3	7.3	78
Trans World	11.1	5.9	53
United	17.2	13.8	80
American	11.2	7.7	69
Pan American	9.6	2.6	27

assumptions described here, several of the major carriers would be in serious financial trouble.

Note that the three transcontinental carriers (American, Trans World, and United) experience shortages of $3.5 billion, $5.2 billion, and $3.4 billion, respectively. This alone demonstrates that taking a simple industry result is inadequate. These three companies are the backbone of scheduled airline service, and none will even come close to meeting projected capital requirements.

Table 5-2
Capital Needs by Carrier with Positive Factors Operative except Leverage
(Debt-to-Equity = 55/45)
(billions of dollars)

Carrier	Capital Requirements	Capital Availability	Percentage of Requirements Covered
Delta	7.7	12.8	166
Braniff	2.9	5.2	179
Northwest	6.6	11.3	171
Continental	2.3	3.6	157
National	2.9	3.3	114
Western	3.0	3.3	110
Eastern	9.3	7.3	78
United	17.2	9.5	55
Trans World	11.1	5.9	53
American	11.2	4.9	44
Pan American	9.6	2.6	27

Appendix A
Operating Passenger Fleets (December 31, 1976)

Table A-1

American Airlines Aircraft in Operation, December 31, 1976

Aircraft Number	Year Acquired	Type Aircraft	Seating
7501	1958	B-707	138
7503	,,	,,	,,
7504	1959	,,	,,
7505	,,	,,	,,
7507	,,	,,	,,
7508	,,	,,	,,
7509	,,	,,	,,
7512	,,	,,	,,
7513	,,	,,	,,
7515	,,	,,	,,
7517	,,	,,	,,
7518	,,	,,	,,
7521	,,	,,	,,
7522	,,	,,	,,
7524	,,	,,	,,
7525	,,	,,	,,
7526	1961	,,	,,
7550	1965	,,	,,
7551	,,	,,	,,
7552	,,	,,	,,
7553	,,	,,	,,
7554	1966	,,	139
7570	,,	,,	,,
7571	,,	,,	138
7572	,,	,,	,,
7573	,,	,,	,,
7574	,,	,,	,,
7575	1967	,,	,,
7578	,,	,,	138
7579	,,	,,	,,
7580	,,	,,	,,
7581	,,	,,	139
7582	,,	,,	138
7583	,,	,,	,,
7584	,,	,,	,,
7585	,,	,,	,,
7586	,,	,,	,,
7587	,,	,,	,,
7588	,,	,,	139
7589	,,	,,	138
7590	,,	,,	139
7591	1968	,,	138

Table A-1 continued

Aircraft Number	Year Acquired	Type Aircraft	Seating
7595	1967	,,	150
7596	,,	,,	147
7597	,,	,,	,,
7598	,,	,,	,,
7599	1967	B-707	149
8401	,,		150
8402	,,		147
8403	,,		150
8404	1968		173
8405	,,		150
8406	,,		,,
9674	1971	B-747	424
1901	1965	B-727-100	100
1902	1966	,,	,,
1903	,,	,,	,,
1905	,,	,,	,,
1906	,,	,,	,,
1907	,,	,,	,,
1908	,,	,,	,,
1909	,,	,,	,,
1910	,,	,,	,,
1928	,,	,,	,,
1929	,,	,,	,,
1930	,,	,,	,,
1931	,,	,,	,,
1932	1967	,,	,,
1933	,,	,,	,,
1934	,,	,,	,,
1935	,,	,,	,,
1955	,,	,,	,,
1956	,,	,,	,,
1957	,,	,,	,,
1958	,,	,,	,,
1959	,,	,,	,,
1962	,,	,,	,,
1964	1968	,,	,,
1965	,,	,,	,,
1969	,,	,,	,,
1970	1964	,,	,,
1971	,,	,,	,,
1972	,,	,,	,,
1973	,,	,,	,,
1974	,,	,,	,,
1975	,,	,,	,,
1976	,,	,,	,,
1977	1964	,,	,,
1978	,,	,,	,,
1979	,,	,,	,,
1980	,,	,,	,,
1981	1964	B-727-100	100
1982	,,	,,	100
1983	,,	,,	,,

Table A-1 continued

Aircraft Number	Year Acquired	Type Aircraft	Seating
1984	,,	,,	,,
1985	1964	,,	,,
1986	1965	,,	,,
1987	,,	,,	,,
1988	,,	,,	,,
1989	,,	,,	,,
1990	,,	,,	,,
1991	,,	,,	,,
1992	,,	,,	,,
1993	,,	,,	,,
1994	,,	,,	,,
1995	,,	,,	,,
1997	,,	,,	,,
1998	1965	,,	,,
2913	1968	,,	,,
2914	,,	,,	,,
6827	1969	B-727-200	125
6828	,,	,,	127
6829	,,	,,	125
6830	,,	,,	,,
6831	,,	,,	,,
6832	,,	,,	127
6833	,,	,,	125
6834	,,	,,	,,
6835	,,	,,	,,
6836	,,	,,	,,
102	1972	DC-10	240
103	1971	,,	,,
104	,,	,,	,,
105	,,	,,	,,
108	1972	,,	,,
109	,,	,,	,,
110	,,	,,	,,
111	,,	,,	,,
112	,,	,,	,,
113	,,	,,	,,
114	,,	,,	,,
115	,,	,,	,,
116	,,	,,	,,
117	,,	,,	,,
118	,,	,,	,,
119	,,	,,	,,
120	1972	DC-10	240
121	,,	,,	,,
122	,,	,,	,,
8431	1969	B-707	150
8432	,,	,,	,,
8433	,,	,,	,,
8434	,,	,,	,,
8435	,,	,,	,,
8436	,,	,,	,,

Table A-1 continued

Aircraft Number	Year Acquired	Type Aircraft	Seating
8437	,,	,,	,,
8438	,,	,,	,,
8439	,,	,,	149
8440	,,	,,	173
8408	1968	,,	147
8409	,,	,,	173
8410	,,	,,	173
8411	,,	,,	150
8412	,,	,,	149
8413	,,	,,	147
8414	,,	,,	173
8415	,,	,,	,,
8416	,,	,,	,,
7592	1969	B-707	138
7593	,,	,,	,,
7594	,,	,,	,,
101	1972	DC-10	240
106	1971	,,	,,
107	,,	,,	,,
123	1972	,,	,,
124	,,	,,	,,
125	,,	,,	,,
2915	1968	B-727/100	100
9670	190	B-747	340
9663	,,	,,	424
9664	,,	,,	,,
9665	,,	,,	340
9666	,,	,,	,,
9667	,,	,,	,,
9669	,,	,,	,,
6800	1968	B-727/200	127
6801	,,	,,	125
6802	,,	,,	,,
6803	,,	,,	127
6804	1968	B-727/200	127
6805	,,	,,	,,
6806	,,	,,	125
6807	,,	,,	127
6808	,,	,,	,,
6809	,,	,,	,,
6810	,,	,,	,,
6811	,,	,,	,,
6812	,,	,,	,,
6813	,,	,,	,,
6814	,,	,,	,,
6815	,,	,,	,,
6816	,,	,,	,,
6817	,,	,,	,,
6818	,,	,,	,,

Table A-1 continued

Aircraft Number	Year Acquired	Type Aircraft	Seating
6819	,,	,,	,,
6820	,,	,,	,,
6821	,,	,,	,,
6822	1969	,,	,,
6823	,,	,,	,,
6824	,,	,,	,,
6825	,,	,,	,,
6826	,,	,,	,,
6837	,,	,,	125
6838	,,	,,	127
6939	,,	,,	125
6841	,,	,,	127
6842	,,	,,	125
843	1975	,,	127
844	,,	,,	125
845	,,	,,	,,
846	,,	,,	127
847	,,	,,	,,
848	,,	,,	,,
849	1976	,,	,,
850	,,	,,	,,
851	,,	,,	,,
852	,,	,,	,,
853	,,	,,	,,
854	,,	,,	,,
856	,,	,,	,,
857	,,	,,	,,
858	,,	,,	,,

Table A-2
Braniff International Corporation Aircraft in Operation December 31, 1976

Aircraft Number	Year Acquired	Type Aircraft	Seating
434	1975	B-727/200	130
435	,,	,,	,,
436	.,	,,	,,
437	,,	,,	,,
438	,,	,,	,,
439	,,	,,	,,
440	1975	,,	,.
441	1976	,,	,,
442	,,	,,	,,
443	,,	,,	,,
444	,,	,,	,,
445	,,	,,	,,
446	,,	,,	,,
447	.,	,,	,,
448	.,	,,	,,
811	1973	DC-8/51	150
812	,,	,,	,,
813	,,	,,	,,
814	,,	,,	,,
297	1969	B-727/100	102
298	,,	,,	,,
299	,,	,,	,,
300	,,	,,	,,
301	.,	,,	,,
309	1972	.,	,,
401	1970	B-727/200	130
402	,,	,,	,,
403	,,	,,	,,
404	1971	,,	,,
405	,,	,,	,,
308	1972	B-727/100	102
7275	1966	,,	,,
7276	,,	,,	,,
7277	.,	,,	,,
7278	1967	,,	,,
7279	,,	,,	,,
7280	,,	,,	,,
7281	,,	,,	,,
7284	,,	,,	,,
7286	,,	,,	,,
7288	,,	,,	,,
7287	.,	,,	,,
7295	,,	,,	,,
7296	,,	,,	,,
9282	,,	,,	,,
7289	,,	,,	,,
7290	,,	,,	,,
7292	,,	,,	,,
7294	,,	,,	,,

Table A-2 continued

Aircraft Number	Year Acquired	Type Aircraft	Seating
406	1972	B-727/200	130
407	,,	,,	,,
408	,,	,,	,,
409	,,	,,	,,
410	,,	,,	,,
411	,,	,,	,,
412	,,	,,	,,
413	,,	,,	,,
414	1973	,,	,,
415	,,	,,	,,
416	,,	,,	,,
417	,,	,,	,,
418	,,	,,	,,
419	,,	,,	,,
420	,,	,,	,,
421	,,	,,	,,
422	,,	,,	,,
423	,,	,,	,,
424	,,	,,	,,
425	,,	,,	,,
426	,,	,,	,,
427	,,	,,	,,
428	,,	,,	,,
429	1974	,,	,,
430	,,	,,	,,
431	,,	,,	,,
432	,,	,,	,,
433	,,	,,	,,

Table A-3
Continental Airlines Aircraft in Operation December 31, 1976

Aircraft Number	Year Acquired	Type Aircraft	Seating
2475	1969	B-727/100	111
2476	1972	,,	,,
18477	1976	,,	108
18478	,,	,,	,,
68041	1972	DC-10	223
68042	,,	,,	,,
68043	,,	,,	,,
68044	,,	,,	,,
68045	,,	,,	,,
68046	1973	,,	203
68047	,,	,,	,,
68048	,,	,,	,,
68049	1974	,,	,,
68050	,,	,,	,,
68051	,,	,,	,,
68052	,,	,,	,,
68053	1975	,,	,,
68054	,,	,,	,,
68055	,,	,,	,:
68056	,,	,,	,,
88701	1968	B-727/200	128
88702	,,	,,	,,
88703	,,	,,	,,
88704	,,	,,	129
88705	,,	,,	128
88706	,,	,,	,,
88707	,,	,,	,,
88708	,,	,,	,,
88709	,,	,,	,,
88710	,,	,,	,,
88711	,,	,,	,,
88712	,,	,,	,,
88713	,,	,,	,,
88714	1969	,,	,,
88715	1970	,,	,,
32716	1970	,,	128
32717	,,	,,	,,
32718	,,	,,	,,
32719	,,	,,	,,
32721	1972	,,	,,
32722	,,	,,	,,
32723	,,	,,	,,
32724	1973	,,	,,
32725	,,	,,	,,
32726	1973	B-727/200	128
24728	,,	,,	,,
25729	,,	,,	,,
25730	,,	,,	,,

Table A-3 continued

Aircraft Number	Year Acquired	Type Aircraft	Seating
66731	1973	,,	,,
66732	1974	,,	,,
66733	,,	,,	,,
66734	,,	,,	,,
66735	,,	,,	,,
66736	1975	,,	,,
66738	,,	,,	,,
66739	,,	,,	,,
66740	,,	,,	,,
231	1975	Rockwell Sabreliner	10

Table A-4
Delta Airlines Aircraft in Operation December 31, 1976

Aircraft Number	Year Acquired	Type Aircraft	Seating
9897	1970	B-747	370
9899	,,	,,	,,
9900	,,	,,	,,
3318	1967	DC-9	90
3319	,,	,,	,,
3320	,,	,,	,,
3321	,,	,,	,,
3324	,,	,,	,,
3325	,,	,,	,,
3326	,,	,,	,,
3327	1968	,,	,,
3328	,,	,,	,,
3329	,,	,,	,,
3330	,,	,,	,,
3331	,,	,,	,,
3332	,,	,,	,,
3333	,,	,,	,,
3334	,,	,,	,,
3335	,,	,,	,,
3336	,,	,,	,,
3337	,,	,,	,,
3338	,,	,,	,,
3339	,,	,,	,,
3340	,,	,,	,,
3341	,,	,,	,,
3342	,,	,,	,,
1261	,,	,,	,,
1262	,,	,,	,,
1263	,,	,,	,,
1264	,,	,,	,,
1265	,,	,,	,,
1266	,,	,,	,,
1267	,,	,,	,,
1268	,,	,,	,,
1269	,,	,,	,,
1270	,,	,,	,,
1271	1969	,,	,,
1272	,,	,,	,,
1273	,,	,,	,,
1274	,,	,,	,,
1275	,,	,,	,,
1276	,,	,,	,,
1277	,,	,,	,,
1278	,,	,,	,,
1279	,,	,,	,,
1280	,,	,,	,,
1281	,,	,,	,,
1282	,,	,,	,,
1283	1969	,,	90
1284	,,	,,	,,

Table A-4 continued

Aircraft Number	Year Acquired	Type Aircraft	Seating
1285	,,	,,	,,
1286	1970	,,	,,
1287	,,	,,	,,
1288	,,	,,	,,
1289	,,	,,	,,
1290	,,	,,	,,
1291	,,	,,	,,
1292	1971	,,	,,
1293	,,	,,	,,
1294	,,	,,	,,
1295	,,	,,	,,
1631	1976	B-727/100	97
1632	,,	,,	,,
1633	,,	,,	,,
1635	,,	,,	,,
1636	,,	,,	,,
701	1973	L-1011	256
702	,,	,,	,,
703	,,	,,	,,
704	,,	,,	,,
705	1974	,,	,,
706	,,	,,	,,
707	,,	,,	,,
708	,,	,,	,,
709	,,	,,	,,
710	,,	,,	,,
711	,,	,,	,,
712	,,	,,	,,
713	,,	,,	,,
714	,,	,,	,,
715	,,	,,	,,
716	,,	,,	,,
717	,,	,,	,,
718	,,	,,	,,
719	1976	,,	,,
720	,,	,,	,,
721	,,	,,	,,
8008	1967	DC-8/51	135
801	1959	,,	,,
803	,,	,,	,,
804	,,	,,	,,
805	,,	,,	,,
806	,,	,,	,,
807	1962	,,	,,
808	,,	,,	,,
809	,,	,,	,,
811	,,	,,	,,
813	1964	,,	,,
814	,,	,,	,,

Table A-4 continued

Aircraft Number	Year Acquired	Type Aircraft	Seating
815	1964	,,	,,
816	1965	,,	,,
817	,,	,,	,,
818	,,	,,	,,
821	1966	,,	,,
400	1975	B-727/200	135
401	,,	,,	,,
402	,,	,,	,,
403	,,	,,	,,
404	,,	,,	,,
405	,,	,,	,,
406	,,	,,	,,
407	,,	,,	,,
408	1976	,,	,,
409	,,	,,	,,
410	,,	,,	,,
411	,,	,,	,,
412	,,	,,	,,
413	,,	,,	,,
414	,,	,,	,,
415	,,	,,	,,
416	,,	,,	,,
417	,,	,,	,,
452	1973	,,	,,
453	,,	,,	,,
454	,,	,,	,,
455	,,	,,	,,
456	,,	,,	,,
457	,,	,,	,,
458	,,	,,	,,
459	,,	,,	,,
460	,,	,,	,,
461	,,	,,	,,
462	,,	,,	,,
463	1973	B-727/200	135
464	,,	,,	,,
465	,,	,,	,,
466	,,	,,	,,
467	,,	,,	,,
468	,,	,,	,,
469	,,	,,	,,
470	,,	,,	,,
471	,,	,,	,,
472	,,	,,	,,
473	,,	,,	,,
474	1974	,,	,,
475	,,	,,	,,
476	,,	,,	,,
477	,,	,,	,,
478	,,	,,	,,
479	,,	,,	,,
480	,,	,,	,,
481	,,	,,	,,

Table A-4 continued

Aircraft Number	Year Acquired	Type Aircraft	Seating
482	,,	,,	,,
483	,,	,,	,,
484	,,	,,	,,
485	,,	,,	,,
486	,,	,,	,,
487	,,	,,	,,
488	1975	,,	,,
489	,,	,,	,,
490	,,	,,	,,
491	,,	,,	,,
492	,,	,,	,,
493	,,	,,	,,
494	,,	,,	,,
495	,,	,,	,,
496	,,	,,	,,
497	,,	,,	,,
498	,,	,,	,,
499	,,	,,	,,
1639	1976	,,	,,
1640	,,	,,	,,
1641	,,	,,	,,
1642	,,	,,	,,
1643	,,	,,	,,
1644	,,	,,	,,
822	1967	DC-8/61	199
823	,,	,,	,,
824	1967	DC-8/61	199
825	1968	,,	,,
826	,,	,,	,,
1300	,,	,,	,,
1301	,,	,,	,,
1302	1969	,,	,,
1303	,,	,,	,,
1304	,,	,,	,,
1305	,,	,,	,,
1306	,,	,,	,,
1307	,,	,,	,,
820	1966	DC-8/51	135
1645	1972	B-727/200	135
1646	,,	,,	,,
1647	,,	,,	,,
1648	,,	,,	,,
1649	,,	,,	,,
1650	,,	,,	,,
1651	,,	,,	,,

Table A-5
Eastern Airlines Aircraft in Operation December 31, 1976

Aircraft Number	Year Acquired	Type Aircraft	Seating
8101	1964	B-727/100	107
8102	1963	”	”
8103	”	”	”
8104	1964	”	”
8105	”	”	”
8106	”	”	”
8107	”	”	”
8108	”	”	”
8109	”	”	”
8110	”	”	”
8111	”	”	”
8112	1974	”	105
8113	”	”	”
8114	”	”	”
8115	”	”	”
8116	”	”	”
8117	”	”	107
8119	1964	”	”
8120	”	”	”
8121	”	”	”
8122	”	”	105
8123	”	”	107
8124	”	”	105
8125	1965	”	”
8126	”	”	”
8127	”	”	”
8128	”	”	”
8129	”	”	”
8130	”	”	”
8131	”	”	”
8132	”	”	”
8133	”	”	”
8134	”	”	107
8135	”	”	”
8136	1973	”	105
8137	”	”	”
8138	”	”	”
8139	”	”	”
8140	”	”	”
8141	1965	”	107
8142	”	”	105
8143	1966	”	”
8147	”	”	”
8148	”	”	”
8149	”	”	”
8150	”	”	”
8151	”	”	”
8152	”	”	”
8153	1966	B-727/100	105
8154	1967	”	107
8155	”	”	105

Table A-5 continued

Aircraft Number	Year Acquired	Type Aircraft	Seating
8156	,,	,,	,,
8157	,,	,,	,,
8158	,,	,,	,,
8159	,,	,,	,,
8160	,,	,,	98
8161	,,	,,	,,
8162	,,	,,	,,
8163	,,	,,	,,
8164	,,	,,	,,
8165	,,	,,	,,
8166	,,	,,	,,
8167	,,	,,	,,
8168	1968	,,	,,
8169	,,	,,	,,
8170	,,	,,	107
8171	,,	,,	105
8172	,,	,,	,,
8836	1970	B-727/200	132
8837	,,	,,	,,
8838	,,	,,	137
8839	,,	,,	,,
8840	,,	,,	132
8841	,,	,,	137
8842	,,	,,	,,
8843	,,	,,	,,
8844	,,	,,	,,
8848	,,	,,	132
8846	,,	,,	,,
8847	,,	,,	,,
8849	,,	,,	,,
8850	,,	,,	,,
8851	1972	,,	137
8852	,,	,,	132
8853	,,	,,	,,
8855	,,	,,	137
8856	,,	,,	,,
8857	,,	,,	132
8858	,,	,,	137
8859	,,	,,	132
8860	1973	,,	,,
8861	,,	,,	,,
8862	,,	,,	137
8863	,,	,,	,,
8864	1973	B-727/200	137
8865	,,	,,	132
8866	,,	,,	,,
8916	1967	DC-9/30	92
8917	1975	,,	,,
8918	,,	,,	105
8919	,,	,,	92
8920	,,	,,	,,
8921	,,	,,	,,

Table A-5 continued

Aircraft Number	Year Acquired	Type Aircraft	Seating
8922	,,	,,	105
8923	,,	,,	,,
8924	,,	,,	,,
8925	,,	,,	,,
8926	,,	,,	,,
8927	1967	,,	,,
8928	,,	,,	,,
8929	,,	,,	92
8930	,,	,,	,,
8931	,,	,,	,,
8932	,,	,,	,,
8933	,,	,,	,,
8934	1968	,,	,,
8935	,,	,,	,,
8936	,,	,,	,,
8937	,,	,,	,,
8938	,,	,,	,,
8939	,,	,,	,,
8940	,,	,,	,,
8941	,,	,,	,,
8942	,,	,,	,,
8943	,,	,,	,,
8944	,,	,,	,,
8945	,,	,,	,,
8946	,,	,,	,,
8947	,,	,,	,,
8948	,,	,,	,,
8949	,,	,,	,,
8950	,,	,,	,,
8951	,,	,,	,,
8952	,,	,,	,,
8953	,,	,,	,,
8954	,,	,,	,,
8955	,,	,,	,,
8956	,,	,,	,,
8957	,,	,,	,,
8958	,,	,,	,,
8959	1968	DC-9/30	92
8960	,,	,,	,,
302	1973	L-1011	268
304	1972	,,	,,
305	,,	,,	,,
306	,,	,,	,,
311	,,	,,	,,
314	1973	,,	,,
316	,,	,,	,,
317	,,	,,	,,
320	,,	,,	,,
321	,,	,,	,,
323	,,	,,	,,
324	,,	,,	,,
325	,,	,,	,,
326	,,	,,	,,

Table A-5 continued

Aircraft Number	Year Acquired	Type Aircraft	Seating
331	1975	"	"
332	"	"	289
333	1976	"	"
334	"	"	268
5504	1958	L-188-08A	82
5507	"	"	"
5511	1959	"	94
5512	1958	"	82
5516	1959	"	94
5517	"	"	82
5518	"	"	94
5522	"	"	87
5523	"	"	92
5525	"	"	87
5528	"	"	"
5529	"	"	"
5534	"	"	"
5535	"	"	"
8901	1971	DC-9/10	67
8908	1966	"	"
8909	"	"	"
8910	"	"	"
8911	"	"	"
8912	"	"	"
8913	"	"	"
8914	"	"	"
8915	"	"	"
8988	1976	DC-9/30	92
8989	"	"	"
8962	1968	DC-9/30	92
8963	"	"	"
8964	"	"	"
8965	"	"	"
8966	"	"	"
8968	"	"	"
8969	"	"	"
8970	"	"	"
8971	"	"	"
8972	"	"	"
8973	"	"	"
8974	"	"	"
8975	"	"	"
8976	"	"	"
8977	"	"	"
8978	"	"	"
8980	"	"	"
8981	"	"	"
8982	"	"	"
8983	1969	"	"
8985	"	"	"

Table A-5 continued

Aircraft Number	Year Acquired	Type Aircraft	Seating
8986	,,	,,	,,
8987	,,	,,	,,
8990	1973	,,	,,
8762- 8766:	subleased to carriers not in this study.		
8173	1968	B-727/100	105
8174	,,	,,	,,
8175	,,	,,	,,
8825	1969	B-727/200	137
8826	,,	,,	,,
8827	,,	,,	,,
8828	,,	,,	,,
8829	,,	,,	137
8830	,,	,,	132
8831	,,	,,	,,
8832	,,	,,	137
8833	,,	,,	132
8834	,,	,,	,,
8835	,,	,,	,,
8867	1973	B-727/200	132
8869	,,	,,	,,
301	1973	L-1011	268
303	1972	,,	,,
308	,,	,,	,,
309	,,	,,	,,
313	,,	,,	,,
318	1973	,,	,,
319	,,	,,	,,
322	,,	,,	,,
327	,,	,,	,,
329	1974	,,	,,
330	1975	,,	,,
312	1973	,,	269
315	,,	,,	,,
8870	1976	B-727/200	137
8871	,,	,,	,,
8872	,,	,,	,,
8873	,,	,,	,,
8874	,,	,,	,,
8875	,,	,,	,,

Table A-6
National Airlines Aircraft in Operation, December 31, 1976

Aircraft Number	Year Acquired	Type Aircraft	Seating
4610	1964	B-727/100	107
4611	,,	,,	,,
4612	,,	,,	,,
4613	,,	,,	,,
4614	1965	,,	,,
4615	,,	,,	,,
4616	,,	,,	,,
4617	,,	,,	,,
4618	,,	,,	,,
4619	,,	,,	,,
4620	1966	,,	,,
4621	,,	,,	,,
4622	,,	,,	,,
4730	1967	B-727/200	136
4731	,,	,,	,,
4732	,,	,,	,,
4733	1968	,,	,,
4734	,,	,,	,,
4735	,,	,,	,,
4736	,,	,,	,,
4737	,,	,,	,,
4738	,,	,,	,,
4739	,,	,,	,,
4740	,,	,,	,,
4741	,,	,,	,,
4742	,,	,,	,,
4743	,,	,,	,,
4744	,,	,,	,,
4745	,,	,,	,,
4746	,,	,,	,,
4747	1965	,,	,,
4748	1968	,,	,,
4749	,,	,,	,,
4750	,,	,,	,,
4751	,,	,,	,,
4752	,,	,,	,,
4753	,,	,,	,,
4754	,,	,,	,,
60	1971	DC-10	270
61	,,	,,	,,
62	,,	,,	,,
63	1972	,,	,,
64	,,	,,	,,
65	,,	,,	,,
66	,,	,,	,,
67	1972	DC-10	270
68	,,	,,	,,
69	1975	,,	,,
70	,,	,,	,,

Table A-6 continued

Aircraft Number	Year Acquired	Type Aircraft	Seating
80	1973	,,	286
81	,,	,,	,,
82	1975	,,	,,
83	,,	,,	,,

Table A-7
Northwest Airlines Aircraft in Operation, December 31, 1976

Aircraft Number	Year Acquired	Type Aircraft	Seating
141	1973	DC-10	236
142	''	''	''
143	1972	''	''
144	''	''	''
145	1973	''	''
146	''	''	''
147	''	''	''
148	''	''	''
149	''	''	''
150	''	''	''
151	''	''	''
152	''	''	''
153	''	''	''
154	''	''	''
155	''	''	''
156	1974	''	''
157	''	''	''
158	''	''	''
159	''	''	''
160	''	''	''
161	''	''	''
162	''	''	''
251	1968	B-727/200	128
252	''	''	''
253	''	''	''
254	''	''	''
255	''	''	''
256	''	''	''
257	''	''	''
258	''	''	''
259	1969	''	''
260	''	''	''
261	''	''	''
262	''	''	''
263	''	''	''
264	''	''	''
265	''	''	''
266	''	''	''
267	''	''	''
268	''	''	''
269	''	''	''
270	''	''	''
271	''	''	''
272	''	''	''
273	''	''	''
275	1975	''	''
276	1975	B-727/200	128
277	''	''	''
278	''	''	''

Table A-7 continued

Aircraft Number	Year Acquired	Type Aircraft	Seating
279	,,	,,	,,
280	,,	,,	,,
281	,,	,,	,,
282	,,	,,	,,
377	1968	B-707/300	165
378	,,	,,	,,
379	,,	,,	,,
380	,,	,,	,,
381	,,	,,	,,
384	,,	,,	,,
385	,,	,,	,,
386	,,	,,	,,
461	1964	B-727/100	93
462	,,	,,	,,
463	,,	,,	,,
464	1965	,,	,,
465	,,	,,	,,
466	,,	,,	,,
467	,,	,,	,,
468	,,	,,	,,
469	,,	,,	,,
470	,,	,,	,,
471	,,	,,	,,
472	,,	,,	,,
473	,,	,,	,,
474	,,	,,	,,
475	1966	,,	,,
476	,,	,,	,,
477	,,	,,	,,
478	,,	,,	,,
479	1967	,,	,,
480	,,	,,	,,
488	1968	,,	,,
489	,,	,,	,,
490	1966	,,	,,
491	,,	,,	,,
492	,,	,,	,,
493	,,	,,	,,
494	,,	,,	,,
495	,,	,,	,,
496	1967	B-727/100	93
497	,,	,,	,,
498	,,	,,	,,
499	,,	,,	,,
601	1970	B-747	369
602	,,	,,	,,
603	,,	,,	,,
604	,,	,,	,,
605	,,	,,	,,
606	,,	,,	,,
607	,,	,,	,,

Table A-7 continued

Aircraft Number	Year Acquired	Type Aircraft	Seating
608	,,	,,	,,
609	,,	,,	,,
610	,,	,,	,,
611	1971	,,	,,
612	,,	,,	,,
613	,,	,,	,,
614	,,	,,	,,
615	,,	,,	,,
620	1976	,,	,,
621.	,,	,,	,,

Table A-8
Pan American World Airways Aircraft in Operation, December 31, 1976

Aircraft Number	Year Acquired	Aircraft Type	Seating
447	1967	B-707	187
448	,,	,,	,,
449	,,	,,	,,
452	,,	,,	,,
459	,,	,,	,,
473	1968	,,	,,
790	1964	,,	,,
791	,,	,,	,,
793	,,	,,	,,
401	1965	,,	,,
402	,,	,,	,,
403	,,	,,	,,
404	,,	,,	,,
405	,,	,,	,,
406	,,	,,	,,
408	,,	,,	,,
409	,,	,,	,,
410	,,	,,	,,
412	,,	,,	,,
414	1966	,,	,,
415	,,	,,	,,
418	,,	,,	,,
419	,,	,,	,,
421	,,	,,	,,
422	1967	,,	,,
423	,,	,,	,,
424	,,	,,	,,
425	,,	,,	,,
426	,,	,,	,,
427	,,	,,	,,
428	,,	,,	,,
433	,,	,,	,,
434	,,	,,	,,
435	,,	,,	,,
453	,,	,,	,,
455	1968	,,	,,
491	,,	,,	,,
492	,,	,,	,,
493	,,	,,	,,
882	,,	,,	,,
883	,,	,,	,,
884	1969	,,	,,
886	,,	,,	,,
887	,,	,,	,,
892	,,	,,	,,
893	,,	,,	,,
894	,,	,,	,,
895	1969	B-707	187
896	,,	,,	,,
897	,,	,,	,,
319	1966	B-727/21	128

Table A-8 continued

Aircraft Number	Year Acquired	Type Aircraft	Seating
323	,,	,,	,,
325	,,	,,	,,
327	,,	,,	,,
329	,,	,,	,,
355	1967	,,	,,
356	,,	,,	,,
357	,,	,,	,,
358	,,	,,	,,
359	,,	,,	,,
360	,,	B-727/21	,,
339	1966	B-727/210	,,
340	,,	,,	,,
652	1971	B-747	362
653	,,	B-747	,,
654	,,	,,	,,
655	,,	,,	,,
733	1969	,,	,,
734	,,	,,	,,
735	1970	,,	,,
736	,,	,,	,,
737	,,	,,	,,
738	,,	,,	,,
739	,,	,,	,,
740	,,	,,	,,
741	,,	,,	,,
742	,,	,,	,,
743	,,	,,	,,
744	,,	,,	,,
747	,,	,,	,,
495	1968	B-707	187
496	,,	,,	,,
497	,,	,,	,,
880	,,	,,	,,
881	,,	,,	,,
885	1969	,,	,,
656	1971	B-747	362
657	,,	,,	,,
659	1973	,,	,,
731	1970	,,	,,
732	,,	,,	,,
748	,,	,,	,,
749	,,	,,	,,
750	1970	B-747	362
751	,,	,,	,,
753	,,	,,	,,
754	,,	,,	,,
755	,,	,,	,,
770	1970	,,	,,
530	1976	,,	,,
531	,,	,,	,,
532	,,	,,	,,
533	,,	,,	,,
534	,,	,,	,,

Table A-9
Trans World Airlines Aircraft in Operation, December 31, 1976

Aircraft Number	Year Acquired	Type Aircraft	Seating
762	1960	B-707	145
763	,,	,,	178
764	,,	,,	,,
767	,,	,,	145
770	,,	,,	178
772	,,	,,	,,
765	,,	,,	145
766	,,	,,	,,
768	,,	,,	,,
771	,,	,,	178
94314	1969	B-727/231	127
64315	,,	,,	,,
54333	1971	,,	,,
54334	,,	,,	,,
54335	,,	,,	,,
54336	,,	,,	,,
54337	,,	,,	,,
54338	1974	,,	,,
64339	,,	,,	,,
54340	,,	,,	,,
746	1962	B-707	127
747	,,	,,	,,
748	,,	,,	,,
749	,,	,,	,,
750	,,	,,	,,
751	,,	,,	,,
752	,,	,,	,,
754	,,	,,	,,
755	,,	,,	,,
756	,,	,,	,,
758	,,	,,	,,
759	,,	,,	,,
781	,,	,,	,,
782	,,	,,	,,
6720	1966	,,	127
6721	,,	,,	,,
6722	,,	,,	,,
6723	,,	,,	,,
6724	,,	,,	,,
86740	1969	,,	,,
86741	,,	,,	,,
783	1962	,,	127
784	,,	,,	,,
785	1962	B-707	127
795	1964	,,	,,
796	,,	,,	,,
797	,,	,,	,,
798	,,	,,	,,

Table A-9 continued

Aircraft Number	Year Acquired	Type Aircraft	Seating
799	,,	,,	,,
6726	1967	,,	,,
6728	,,	,,	,,
6727	,,	,,	,,
6729	,,	,,	,,
6763	,,	,,	,,
6764	,,	,,	,,
6771	,,	,,	,,
6789	,,	,,	,,
6790	,,	,,	,,
1793	1970	,,	143
7941	,,	,,	,,
93119	1976	B-747	363
844	1964	B-727/31	93
845	,,	,,	,,
846	,,	,,	,,
847	,,	,,	,,
848	,,	,,	,,
849	,,	,,	,,
850	,,	,,	,,
851	,,	,,	,,
852	,,	,,	,,
853	,,	,,	,,
854	,,	,,	,,
855	,,	,,	,,
856	,,	,,	,,
857	,,	,,	,,
858	,,	,,	,,
7890	1969	B-727/31	93
97891	,,	,,	,,
7892	,,	,,	,,
7893	,,	,,	,,
859	1964	,,	,,
831	1965	,,	,,
833	,,	,,	,,
839	,,	,,	,,
840	,,	,,	,,
841	,,	,,	,,
842	1966	,,	,,
889	1966	B-727/31	93
18702	1966	B-707	145
18703	,,	,,	,,
18704	,,	,,	,,
8705	1965	,,	,,
8730	1969	,,	,,
18706	1966	,,	,,
18707	,,	,,	,,
18708	,,	,,	,,
18709	,,	,,	184
8731	1969	,,	178

Table A-9 continued

Aircraft Number	Year Acquired	Type Aircraft	Seating
8725	1966	,,	145
760	1965	,,	,,
779	,,	,,	,,
780	,,	,,	,,
793	,,	,,	,,
8732	1969	,,	
8729	1968	,,	184
18710	1967	,,	145
18711	,,	,,	,,
18712	,,	,,	184
18713	,,	,,	145
774	1962	,,	,,
28714	1963	,,	,,
773	,,	,,	,,
775	1962	,,	,,
778	1963	,,	,,
890	1967	B-727/31	93
891	,,	,,	,,
892	,,	,,	,,
893	,,	,,	,,
894	,,	,,	,,
895	,,	,,	,,
1055	1966	DC-9	73
1056	,,	,,	,,
1057	,,	,,	,,
1058	,,	,,	,,
1059	,,	,,	,,
1060	,,	,,	,,
1061	,,	,,	,,
1062	,,	,,	,,
1064	1967	,,	,,
1065	,,	,,	,,
1066	,,	,,	,,
1067	,,	,,	,,
1068	1967	DC-9	73
1069	,,	,,	,,
1070	,,	,,	,,
1051	1966	,,	,,
1053	,,	,,	,,
1054	,,	,,	,,
31001	1972	L-1011	230
11002	,,	,,	,,
11003	,,	,,	,,
11004	,,	,,	,,
11005	,,	,,	,,
11006	,,	,,	,,
31008	1973	,,	,,
31013	,,	,,	,,
31014	,,	,,	,,
31015	1974	,,	,,
41016	,,	,,	,,
15017	,,	,,	,,

Table A-9 continued

Aircraft Number	Year Acquired	Type Aircraft	Seating
31018	,,	,,	,,
41020	,,	,,	,,
31024	,,	,,	,,
81025	,,	,,	,,
81026	1975	,,	,,
81027	,,	,,	,,
81028	,,	,,	,,
31029	,,	,,	,,
31030	,,	,,	,,
31031	,,	,,	,,
28724	1968	B-707	145
28726	,,	,,	184
28727	,,	,,	,,
28728	,,	,,	,,
8733	1969	,,	145
8735	,,	,,	,,
8736	,,	,,	,,
8737	,,	,,	,,
8738	,,	,,	,,
16738	1968	B-707	127
16739	,,	,,	,,
9515	,,	B-727	93
9516	,,	,,	,,
12301	,,	,,	127
12302	,,	,,	,,
12303	1968	B-727	127
12304	,,	,,	,,
12305	,,	,,	,,
12306	,,	,,	,,
12307	,,	,,	,,
12308	,,	,,	,,
52309	,,	,,	,,
52310	,,	,,	,,
52311	,,	,,	,,
52312	,,	,,	,,
52313	,,	,,	,,
44316	1969	,,	,,
74317	,,	,,	,,
74318	,,	,,	,,
64319	,,	,,	,,
64320	,,	,,	,,
64321	,,	,,	,,
64322	,,	,,	,,
64323	,,	,,	,,
64324	,,	,,	,,
54325	1970	,,	,,
54326	,,	,,	,,
54327	,,	,,	,,
54329	,,	,,	,,
54330	,,	,,	,,
54331	,,	,,	,,
54332	,,	,,	,,
93104	,,	B-747	363

Table A-9 continued

Aircraft Number	Year Acquired	Type Aircraft	Seating
93105	,,	,,	,,
93106	,,	,,	,,
93107	,,	,,	,,
93108	,,	,,	,,
93109	,,	,,	,,
53110	,,	,,	,,
93115	1971	,,	,,
53116	,,	,,	,,
93117	,,	,,	,,
31009	1973	L-1011	230
31010	,,	,,	,,
31011	,,	,,	,,
41012	,,	,,	,,
31019	1974	,,	,,
31021	,,	,,	,,
31022	,,	,,	,,
31023	,,	,,	,,

Table A-10
United Airlines Aircraft in Operation, December 31, 1976

Aircraft Number	Year Acquired	Type Aircraft	Seating
7620	1968	B-727	96
7621	,,	,,	,,
7622	,,	,,	,,
7623	,,	,,	,,
7624	,,	,,	,,
7625	,,	,,	,,
7626	,,	,,	,,
7627	,,	,,	,,
7628	,,	,,	,,
7629	,,	,,	,,
7630	,,	,,	,,
7631	,,	,,	,,
7632	,,	,,	,,
7633	,,	,,	,,
7634	,,	,,	,,
7635	,,	,,	,,
7636	,,	,,	,,
7637	,,	,,	,,
7638	,,	,,	,,
7639	1969	,,	,,
7640	,,	,,	,,
7641	,,	,,	,,
7642	,,	,,	,,
7643	,,	,,	,,
7647	,,	,,	,,
7001	1964	B-727	96
7002	,,	,,	,,
7004	,,	,,	,,
7005	,,	,,	,,
7006	,,	,,	,,
7007	,,	,,	,,
7008	,,	,,	,,
7009	,,	,,	,,
7010	,,	,,	,,
7011	,,	,,	,,
7012	,,	,,	,,
7013	,,	,,	,,
7014	,,	,,	,,
7015	,,	,,	,,
7016	,,	,,	,,
7017	,,	,,	,,
7018	,,	,,	,,
7019	,,	,,	,,
7020	,,	,,	,,
7021	,,	,,	,,
7022	,,	,,	,,
7023	,,	,,	,,
7024	1964	B-727	96
7025	,,	,,	,,
7026	,,	,,	,,

Table A-10 continued

Aircraft Number	Year Acquired	Type Aircraft	Seating
7027	1965	,,	,,
7054	,,	,,	,,
7055	1966	,,	,,
7056	,,	,,	,,
7057	,,	,,	,,
7058	,,	,,	,,
7059	,,	,,	,,
7060	,,	,,	,,
7061	,,	,,	,,
7062	,,	,,	,,
7063	,,	,:	,,
7065	,,	,,	,,
7066	,,	,,	,,
7068	,,	,,	,,
7069	,,	,,	,,
7078	1968	,,	,,
7079	,,	,,	,,
7080	,,	,,	,,
7081	,,	,,	,,
7082	,,	,,	,,
7090	,,	,,	,,
7116	,,	,,	,,
7117	,,	,,	,,
7118	,,	,,	,,
7119	,,	,,	,,
7120	,,	,,	,,
7121	,,	,,	,,
7122	,,	,,	,,
7123	,,	,,	,,
7124	,,	,,	,,
7126	,,	,,	,,
7127	,,	,,	,,
7128	,,	,,	,,
7129	,,	,,	,,
7130	,,	,,	,,
7131	1968	,,	,,
7132	,,	,,	,,
7133	,,	,,	,,
7135	,,	,,	,,
7136	,,	,,	,,
7137	,,	,,	,,
7138	,,	,,	,,
4713	1970	B-747	342
4714	,,	,,	,,
4716	1970	B-747	342
4717	,,	,,	,,
4718	1971	,,	,,
4719	,,	,,	,,
4720	,,	,,	,,
4723	1972	,,	,,
4727	,,	,,	,,
8001	1960	DC-8	127

Table A-10 continued

Aircraft Number	Year Acquired	Type Aircraft	Seating
8002	1961	,,	,,
8003	1960	,,	,,
8004	1959	,,	,,
8005	,,	,,	,,
8006	,,	,,	,,
8012	,,	,,	,,
8014	,,	,,	,,
8015	,,	,,	,,
8016	,,	,,	,,
8017	,,	,,	,,
8018	1960	,,	,,
8019	1959	,,	,,
8020	1960	,,	,,
8021	,,	,,	,,
8022	,,	,,	,,
8023	,,	,,	,,
8024	,,	,,	,,
8025	,,	,,	,,
8026	,,	,,	,,
8027	,,	,,	,,
8028	,,	,,	,,
8029	,,	,,	,,
8030	,,	,,	,,
8031	,,	,,	,,
8032	,,	,,	,,
8033	,,	,,	,,
8037	1961	,,	,,
8038	,,	,,	,,
8039	,,	,,	,,
1801	1972	DC-10	242
1803	,,	,,	,,
1808	,,	,,	,,
1809	,,	,,	,,
1810	,,	,,	,,
1811	,,	,,	,,
1812	1972	DC-10	242
1813	,,	,,	,,
1814	,,	,,	,,
1815	,,	,,	,,
1816	1973	,,	,,
1819	1974	,,	,,
1820	,,	,,	,,
1821	,,	,,	,,
1822	,,	,,	,,
1823	,,	,,	,,
1824	,,	,,	,,
1825	,,	,,	,,
1826	1975	,,	,,
1827	,,	,,	,,
1828	,,	,,	,,
1829	,,	,,	,,
1830	,,	,,	,,
1831	,,	,,	,,

Table A-10 continued

Aircraft Number	Year Acquired	Type Aircraft	Seating
1832	,,	,,	,,
1833	1972	,,	,,
1834	,,	,,	,,
1836	1973	,,	,,
1837	,,	,,	,,
8070	1967	DC-8	184
8071	,,	,,	,,
8072	1968	,,	,,
8073	1967	,,	,,
8074	,,	,,	,,
8076	,,	,,	,,
8077	1968	,,	,,
8078	,,	,,	,,
8079	,,	,,	,,
8080	,,	,,	,,
8081	,,	,,	,,
8082	,,	,,	,,
8083	,,	,,	223
8084	,,	,,	184
8085	,,	,,	,,
8086	,,	,,	,,
8087	,,	,,	,,
8088	,,	,,	,,
8089	,,	,,	,,
8090	,,	,,	,,
8091	,,	,,	,,
8092	,,	,,	,,
8093	1968	DC-8	184
8094	,,	,,	,,
8966	1969	DC-8	143
8967	,,	,,	,,
8971	,,	,,	173
8975	,,	,,	,,
9001	1969	B-737	95
9002	1967	,,	,,
9003	1968	,,	,,
9004	,,	,,	,,
9006	,,	,,	,,
9007	,,	,,	,,
9008	,,	,,	,,
9009	,,	,,	,,
9010	,,	,,	,,
9011	,,	,,	,,
9012	,,	,,	,,
9013	,,	,,	,,
9014	,,	,,	,,
9015	,,	,,	,,
9016	,,	,,	,,
9017	,,	,,	,,
9018	,,	,,	,,
9019	,,	,,	,,

Table A-10 continued

Aircraft Number	Year Acquired	Type Aircraft	Seating
9020	,,	,,	,,
9021	,,	,,	,,
9022	,,	,,	,,
9023	,,	,,	,,
9024	,,	,,	,,
9025	,,	,,	,,
9026	,,	,,	,,
9027	,,	,,	,,
9028	,,	,,	,,
9030	,,	,,	,,
9032	,,	,,	,,
9033	,,	,,	,,
9038	,,	,,	,,
9039	,,	,,	,,
9040	,,	,,	,,
9043	1969	,,	,,
9044	,,	,,	,,
9045	,,	,,	,,
9046	,,	,,	,,
9047	,,	,,	,,
9048	1969	B-737	95
9050	,,	,,	,,
9051	,,	,,	,,
9052	,,	,,	,,
9053	,,	,,	,,
9054	,,	,,	,,
9057	,,	,,	,,
9060	,,	,,	,,
9061	,,	,,	,,
9062	,,	,,	,,
9063	,,	,,	,,
9065	,,	,,	,,
9066	,,	,,	,,
9067	,,	,,	,,
9068	,,	,,	,,
9069	,,	,,	,,
9070	,,	,,	,,
9071	,,	,,	,,
9072	,,	,,	,,
9075	,,	,,	,,
8007	1959	DC-8	127
8008	,,	,,	,,
8009	,,	,,	,,
8010	,,	,,	,,
8011	,,	,,	,,
8035	1961	,,	,,
8060	1976	,,	,,
8061	,,	,,	,,
8062	,,	,,	,,
8063	,,	,,	,,
8064	,,	,,	,,
8065	,,	,,	,,
8066	1966	,,	154

Table A-10 continued

Aircraft Number	Year Acquired	Type Aircraft	Seating
8067	,,	,,	,,
8068	,,	,,	,,
8069	,,	,,	,,
4704	1970	B-747	342
4703	,,	,,	,,
4710	,,	,,	,,
4711	,,	,,	,,
4712	,,	,,	,,
4723	1973	,,	,,
4729	,,	,,	,,
4732	,,	,,	,,
4735	1973	B-747	342
7003	1965	B-727	96
7028	,,	,,	,,
7029	,,	,,	,,
7031	,,	,,	,,
7032	,,	,,	,,
7033	,,	,,	,,
7034	,,	,,	,,
7035	,,	,,	,,
7037	,,	,,	,,
7038	,,	,,	,,
7039	,,	,,	,,
7040	,,	,,	,,
7041	,,	,,	,,
7042	,,	,,	,,
7044	,,	,,	,,
7045	,,	,,	,,
7046	,,	,,	,,
7047	,,	,,	,,
7048	,,	,,	,,
7049	,,	,,	,,
7050	,,	,,	,,
7052	,,	,,	,,
7053	,,	,,	,,
7064	1966	,,	,,
7067	,,	,,	,,
7070	,,	,,	,,
7071	,,	,,	,,
7072	,,	,,	,,
7073	1967	,,	,,
7074	,,	,,	,,
7075	,,	,,	,,
7076	,,	,,	,,
7077	,,	,,	,,
7083	,,	,,	,,
7084	,,	,,	,,
7085	,,	,,	,,
7086	,,	,,	,,
7087	,,	,,	,,
7088	,,	,,	,,
7089	,,	,,	,,

Table A-10 continued

Aircraft Number	Year Acquired	Type Aircraft	Seating
7101	1966	,,	,,
7102	,,	,,	,,
7103	,,	,,	,,
7104	,,	,,	,,
7105	1966	B-727	96
7106	,,	,,	,,
7107	,,	,,	,,
7108	,,	,,	,,
7109	,,	,,	,,
7110	,,	,,	,,
7111	,,	,,	,,
7112	,,	,,	,,
7113	,,	,,	,,
7114	,,	,,	,,
7115	,,	,,	,,
7644	1969	B-727	126
7645	,,	,,	,,
7646	,,	,,	,,
8075	1967	DC-8	173
8095	1969	,,	184
8096	,,	,,	,,
8097	,,	,,	,,
8098	,,	,,	,,
8099	,,	,,	,,
8968	1969	DC-8	173
8969	,,	,,	,,
8970	,,	,,	,,
8973	,,	,,	,,
8974	,,	,,	,,
1802	1971	DC-10	242
1804	,,	,,	,,
1805	,,	,,	,,
1806	,,	,,	,,
1807	,,	,,	,,
1817	,,	,,	,,
1818	,,	,,	,,
1835	,,	,,	,,
9029	1968	B-737	95

Table A-11
Western Airlines Aircraft in Operation, December 31, 1976

Aircraft Number	Year Acquired	Type Aircraft	Seating
1501	1968	B-707	147
1502	,,	,,	,,
1503	,,	,,	79
1504	,,	,,	147
1505	,,	,,	,,
4501	1968	B-737	99
4502	,,	,,	,,
4503	,,	,,	,,
4505	,,	,,	,,
4507	,,	,,	,,
4508	,,	,,	,,
4509	,,	,,	,,
4510	,,	,,	,,
4511	,,	,,	,,
4512	,,	,,	,,
4513	,,	,,	,,
4514	,,	,,	,,
4515	,,	,,	,,
4516	,,	,,	,,
4517	,,	,,	,,
4518	1969	,,	,,
4519	,,	,,	,,
4520	,,	,,	,,
4521	,,	,,	,,
4523	,,	,,	,,
4526	,,	,,	,,
4528	,,	,,	,,
4530	,,	,,	,,
901	1973	DC-10	254
904	,,	,,	,,
905	1974	,,	,,
2807	1972	B-727	122
2808	,,	,,	,,
2809	,,	,,	,,
2810	,,	,,	,,
2811	,,	,,	,,
2812	1974	,,	,,
2813	,,	,,	,,
2814	,,	,,	,,
2815	,,	,,	,,
2816	,,	,,	,,
2817	,,	,,	,,
2818	,,	,,	,,
2819	1975	,,	,,
2820	,,	,,	,,
2821	1975	B-727	122
93143	1961	B-720	128
93144	,,	,,	,,

Table A-11 continued

Aircraft Number	Year Acquired	Type Aircraft	Seating
93145	1962	"	"
93146	"	"	"
93147	"	"	"
93148	1963	"	"
93149	"	"	"
93153	1965	"	"
93154	"	"	"
93156	"	"	"
93159	1966	"	"
93160	"	"	"
93161	"	"	"
93162	"	"	"
93163	1967	"	"
93164	"	"	"
93165	1967	"	"
93167	"	"	"
2801	1969	B-727	122
2802	"	"	"
2803	"	"	"
2804	"	"	"
2805	"	"	"
2806	"	"	"
902	1973	DC-10	254
903	"	"	"
906	1975	"	"
907	1976	"	"

Appendix B
The Role of Leasing

The Securities and Exchange Commission has long recognized that the omission of financing leases from financial statements has (1) understated the assets required by a corporation to manufacture its product or render its service; (2) understated the amount of the company's long-term debt, thereby enabling the corporation to circumvent restrictions in agreements with lenders; and (3) misstated periodic income.

Over the entire life of the lease, income will be the same regardless of whether or not the lease is capitalized. If the agreement is treated as an operating lease, all the payments will be treated as rental expense. If it is determined that the agreement constitutes a capital lease, the asset acquired is capitalized and depreciated over the life of the lease, the related liability is recorded, and total payments made under the agreement are allocated between interest expense and the amortization of principal indebtedness. Herein lies the basis for inter-period differences on the income statement. A mortgage schedule is characterized by relatively high interest expense and relatively little amortization of principal in the early stages of its tenure. In the latter phase of a mortgage, the relationship reverses itself.

Capitalizing leases therefore reduces income for periods early in the life of the lease, and increases income—often by significant amounts—in the later stages.

In response to the controversy surrounding this financing medium, the now defunct Accounting Principles Board issued no less than four of its regulations (called opinions) to specify guidelines for lessor and lessee disclosure. These regulations did not require the capitalization of financing leases; rather they governed disclosure of various data in the notes to the financial statements.

Financial analysts were generally satisfied with the disclosure so obtained, which included the present value of commitments, future minimum payments by year for five years and then by five year aggregates for twenty-five years, average interest rate implicit in financing leases, and various sub-lease data. The SEC, however, was not fully satisfied.

The successor agency to the Accounting Principles Board, the Financial Accounting Standards Board, has decided to require the capitalization of financing leases. The procedures are detailed in its *Statement of Financial Accounting Standards No. 13*. The parameters for designating a lease as a financing lease (or a capital lease under the new terminology) are as follows:

1. The lease transfers ownership of the property to the lessor at the end of the lease, or if he or she is able to purchase it at a bargain price.
2. The lease term is for 75 percent or more of the life of the leased property, *or*

3. The present value of the lease payments at the inception of the lease equals or exceeds 90 percent of the fair value of the leased asset reduced by the investment tax credit.

Present value is calculated by the lessee using his incremental borrowing rate, unless the lessor's implicit rate of return is estimated to be lower, in which case the lessee calculates the lessor's implicit rate of return as follows:

1. Treats the periodic rental payments as a series of annuities to be received by the lessor. Includes a final period payment equal to the estimated residual value of the property which reverts to the lessor.
2. These payments are considered as the debt incurred to finance the fair market value of the leased asset less any investment tax credit for which the lessor qualifies. ("Debt" is used here to imply the total of interest and principal payments equalling total rentals to be paid.)
3. The lessor's rate is then calculated.

The lessor's implicit rate is then used by the lessee to capitalize the stream of payments (now excluding the residual) as an asset and an obligation on the balance sheet.

Aircraft leasing is now a relatively mature phenomenon. For several carriers, the earnings turn-around point occurs by or before 1980. This implies a significant amount of "paper profits" in the 1980s.

Bibliography

Air Transport Association. *The Sixty Billion Dollar Question.* Washington, D.C.: Air Transport Association, 1976.

Byrne and Kelliher. "The Big Buy," in the *Wall Street Journal,* September 25, 1978.

Civil Aeronautics Board. *Airline Equipment Needs and Financing Through 1985.* Washington, D.C.: Civil Aeronautics Board, 1975.

Civil Aeronautics Board, Financial and Cost Section. *Operating Expenses by Functional Groupings.* Washington, D.C.: Civil Aeronautics Board, 1976.

Connelly, Julie. "TWA: A Company In Search of $3 Billion." *Institutional Investor,* December 1977.

Cook, James. "Pan American: Coming Home." *Forbes,* October 16, 1978.

Douglas, George, and Miller, James. *Economic Regulation Of Domestic Air Transport.* Washington, D.C.: Brookings Institution, 1974.

NASA. *Outlook for Aeronautics.* Virginia: National Technical Information Services, 1976.

O'Connor, William E. *Economic Regulation Of The World's Airlines.* New York: Holt, Rinehart and Winston, 1971.

Smith, Henry Ladd. *Airways Abroad.* Madison: University of Wisconsin Press, 1950.

Thayer, Frederick C. *Air Transport Policy and National Security.* Chapel Hill: University of North Carolina Press, 1965.

United States Federal Aviation Agency. *Report Of The Task Force On Aviation Goals.* Washington, D.C.: Government Printing Office, 1961.

Vose, Allan D., and Kane, Robert M. *Air Transportation.* Dubuque: Kendall/ Hunt Publishing, 1974.

Weller, John L. "Access to Capital Markets," in *The Future Of American Transportation,* E.W. Williams, ed. New Jersey: Prentice Hall, Inc., 1971.

Woolsey, James, and Baumgarner, James. "Airplane Builders Prepare Assault On Economic Barrier," in *Air Transport World,* February 1978.

Woolsey, James. "Uncertainties Cloud U.S. Airplane Programs," in *Air Transport World,* April 1977.

Index

Accounting Principles Board, 153
Airbus, 17, 29-30, 96, 97, 103
Aircraft in operation, 113-151
Aircraft rentals, *see* Leases and leasing practices
Aircraft service life, xvi, 12, 19-20, 25-26, 31, 44, 100; and capital requirements, summaries of, 32-43; and fleet standardization, 98
Air fares, 3, 14; CAB and, 10-11, 12, 13, 89 92; deregulation of, 15, 102, 107, 108, 109, 111; discount, 11; and "no frills" service, 89
Air Force, U.S., 2, 4
Airline mergers, 4, 6, 108, 109
Airmail Acts (1930, 1934), 1-3
Airmail service, 1-3, 4
Air pollution legislation, 75. *See also* Regulatory policies
Airport and Airways Development Act (1970), 5
Airports: government funding of, 4-5
Air Transport Association (ATA), xvi, 9, 11, 13, 14, 19-20, 22, 23
America, *see* Latin America; United States
Americana Hotel Chain, 74
American Airlines, 1, 2, 3, 6, 15, 21 103; aircraft in operation (Dec. 31, 1976), 113-117; capital requirements for, 20, 25-26, 73-75, 85; financial position of, 25-27, 73-75, 85, 95-96, 102, 106-107, 112; and merger, 109; new debt estimates for, 74, 80; and noise control modifications, 24-25; operating expenses of, 85, 90-92, 94-96, 98-99; operating income of, 93-94, 97; operating ratio of, 73, 86, 94; projected operating earnings, 51, 62, 73-74; revenues/yield of, 12, 85, 86, 96, 102; shortage and surplus estimates for, 86; wage and benefit expenses, 75, 85

American Overseas Airlines, 6. *See also* American Airlines
Arnold, Major Henry, 4
Aviation Act (1938), 9

Bermuda Agreement, 5
Boeing Aircraft Company, 45; and acceptance of orders, xvi; aircraft in service, 25, 28, 31, 46; aircraft prices, 21; development of new aircraft by, xvi, 6, 16-17, 103
Braniff, Tom, 2
Braniff Airways, 3, 4
Braniff International Corporation, 91; aircraft in operation (Dec. 31, 1976), 118-119; capital requirements for, 21, 26-27; financial position of, 98, 107; new debt estimates for, 75, 80; operating expenses and ratio of, 85, 96; projected operating earnings for, 52, 63; revenues/yield of, 86, 92, 96; shortage and surplus estimates for, 87
British Airways, 103
Brookings Institution, 11
Brown, Walter (Postmaster General), 2, 4
Bureau of Air Commerce, 3. *See also* Federal Aviation Administration

Canteen Corporation, 101
Capital Airlines, 4
Capital availability, xvi; forecasted, 49-109; periods ending Dec. 31 (1985 and 1989), 105
Capital needs by carrier: all positive factors operative, 112; positive factors operative except leverage, 112
Capital requirement summaries, 20-43
Capital shortage, summary of (1976-1989), 106
Capital structure by airline (Dec. 31, 1976), 50

About the Author

Robert W. Mandell has held responsible positions in many areas of business and academia. He graduated from Fordham University with a B.A. in economics and English in 1971, and an M.A. in economics in 1972. Turning towards business, he completed an M.B.A. in financial accounting at New York University, and a Ph.D. in economics at Fordham.

Dr. Mandell was a staff accountant with Price Waterhouse & Co. (1973-74), and held staff positions in the Accounting and Budget Departments at American Airlines. The interest which triggered the research for this book arose from the high regard he acquired for the industry during this period.

Presently, he is manager of financial systems development for AMF, Inc. His most recent teaching positions have been in M.B.A. programs and in the Graduate Economics Program at Fordham University.